The WEALTH *of* POVERTY

Capitalizing the Opportunities of Poverty for the Kingdom of God

REV. DR. TINA CARTER & REV. DR. MINDY JOHNSON-HICKS

outskirtspress

DENVER, COLORADO

The Wealth of Poverty
Capitalizing the Opportunities of Poverty for the Kingdom of God

Outskirts Press, Inc.
http://www.outskirtspress.com

ISBN: 978-1-4787-2507-7

PRINTED IN THE UNITED STATES OF AMERICA

Table of Contents

Introduction

Capitalizing: To convert into accessible wealth

Poverty is a subject that is often easier to turn away from. This book is our attempt to stop turning away, to grapple meaningfully with the benefits wrought within the culture of poverty and to entice others to become grapplers alongside us. We wish to convert the wealth of poverty into capital that is recognized and accessible to all persons; poor, rich and in between.

In order to grapple meaningfully with poverty in the 18th century, John Wesley, one of the founders of the United Methodist Church, went to where the poor were. He didn't wait for the poor to come to him or to a church. Instead, he went to the fields and mines. John Wesley went out into the cultures; ruling, middle, working and poverty to offer a word of hope and healing. He invited "the poor" to small groups where they could mutually support one another while learning cultural skills that could move them into the working and middle classes. He established the first community health clinics in England and he was one of the most prolific publishers of his time. John Wesley sought to educate and improve conditions for the poor of England. His "methods", hence Methodism, transformed people and unethical systems around the globe.

He also had a problem. John Wesley said as people practiced their faith and frugality and as they learned to behave in cultural consonance with the middle class, they moved into the middle class. Upon finding this upward mobility, they abandoned their community and the other poor people and relationship systems that were an indispensable part of their daily lives not long ago. John Wesley was displeased with these formerly poor middle class folks who were keeping their newly gained wealth and skill for personal gain. Wesley feared the movement he started would rob the soul of God's people by defrauding God of the return of investment on which God should have been able to depend. Wesley preached:

> You have more of the goods of this world than is needful either for yourself or your family...Have you not more money, or more of money's worth, than you had ten or twenty years ago, or at this time last year? Do not you know that God entrusted you with that money (all above what buys necessaries for your families) to feed the hungry, to clothe the naked, to help the stranger, the widow, the fatherless; and, indeed, as far as it will go, to relieve the wants of all mankind? How can you, how dare you, defraud your Lord, by applying it to any other purpose?[1]

John Wesley began with a method for coming to know God which resulted in economic success which, Wesley thought, would return to uplift more poor using the same tried and true method. Today, we find many United Methodist Churches filled with people who care about each other and about God and even some who continue to follow Wesley's methods. We find United Methodist ministries that circle the globe. We've also found a lot of United Methodists who want to "help the poor." This book is an effort to aid people in "helping the poor" by teaching this simple method: It is the poor who own the true wealth, a true wealth which we can only access by interacting with the hungry, the naked, the stranger, the widow, the fatherless, the smelly, the pushy, and the basket cases. Anything less defrauds God. It is a good time to remember, this is Good News.

---

1 http://www.umcmission.org/Find-Resources/John-Wesley-Sermons/Sermon-126-On-the-Danger-of-Increasing-Riches#sthash.NIIQoO9L.dpuf. Public Domain.

Not too long ago, our church was visited by one such faithful United Methodist group. Among them was a woman who had traveled to our location with her granddaughter. It seems that the grandmother had read the book *The Christmas Jar* by Jason Wright.[2] While the intent of the book is to develop a strong sense of selfless giving and to reorient Christmas away from a "want" list and toward "doing good for others," this particular grandmother might have misread the intent. She had a jar in hand filled with coins that they had saved over the year. The idea from the book is to have such a jar in your home and to give it away "anonymously." However, this grandmother had brought the jar and her granddaughter to, "give it to the poor people." When she arrived at our church she asked if we knew any poor people. And, not for the first time, I was frustrated that once again people who were economically secure were using the poor to teach an object lesson to their children about the power of generosity.

I wanted to ask the woman why, if she was a Christian, she didn't know any poor people? I wanted to encourage the woman to meditate on the saying that we are supposed to love people and use things, not love things and use people. Instead, I found one of my friends, who would never label herself as poor but who has been through training on cross-economic relationships and asked her to receive the gift. She did, and was gracious. But my frustration was building. I work in a neighborhood that is a mixture of houses that are middle class with some of the worst apartments in the city. The congregation where I serve is multicultural and multi-economic. I had already started training people all over the country about working "with" the poor (instead of "to", "for", or "at" the poor). And I was becoming more and more frustrated at the depth of the divide in both understanding and actual shared living experiences between the culture of power, the middle class and those in generational poverty. I longed to convert the "wealth of poverty" into wealth that is recognized and accessible to others. I longed for a forum or an educational tool that would help me to explain the wealth of the poor without making other

---

2 Wright, Jason. 2005. Christmas Jars, Shadow Mountain Publishers.

cultures and classes feel threatened. And while I knew that I could provide effective training in person I longed for a systematic way of describing what I was experiencing.

And then God sent Dr. Mindy Johnson-Hicks into my life, an ordained pastor who also has experience in generational poverty. Dr. Johnson-Hicks has a great capacity to organize ideas and describe not only the conditions of poverty but the culture of poverty. She understood that many of the parts of the culture of generational poverty are more "Jesus-y" than other cultural systems. She could describe her understandings without panicking other-class people who might react against the cultural advantages of poverty in their role as gate-keepers of the status quo.

In this book you will find the best of both of us — and, more than that, a systematic demonstration of the wealth of the poverty culture. Chapter one develops an understanding of why God favors the poor and where you can read about that favoritism in the Bible. Chapter two delves into the culture of poverty, helping the reader identify some of the key markers of that culture. Chapter three begins mining the wealth of the culture of poverty as they cope with unforeseen problems through imaginative scheduling. Chapter four highlights the strength developed in the crucible of poverty. Chapter five examines the question of value as the poor often hold valuable things others might not find meaningful. Chapter six exposes the wealth of networking and relationships that drive the community of poverty. Chapter seven highlights the necessity of reliance on others when resources are scarce. At the end of each chapter are questions for reflection which can be considered either personally or with a group. Finally, included as an appendix, is a previously gathered body of stories which were mined from the wealth of poverty in one local congregation.

Our goal is not to romanticize poverty. We believe that God's Kingdom excludes poverty and that working toward God's kingdom here means working with God to eliminate poverty and create a system where everyone has enough. Our goal is simply to describe some Godly lessons which are learned by living in a culture of poverty; like valuing relationships and understanding that interdependence is a good gift from God. Our goal in these pages is to help people who are not familiar with the culture of poverty to gain not only familiarity but, perhaps, appreciation for the culture of poverty. Perhaps that appreciation can lead to a new way of thinking about working and living "with the poor." We believe that only through relationship will the grace of Jesus Christ become real in our lives. Only through relationship will we all be transformed, regardless of class or culture. We hope this book makes the blessings of inter-economic relationships possible so that God might save us all.

CHAPTER 1

God's Favor

God loves the poor. God expects Christ-followers to love the poor. When Christ-followers begin to love the poor, they may begin to see the wealth the poor have to offer.

Psalm 140:12 (NRSV)
[12] I know that the Lord maintains the cause of the needy, and executes justice for the poor.

It may be easy to discount this single verse yanked out of context from a potentially royal Solomonic lamenting prayer. There are certainly other Hebrew Bible references we could draw from here. There are 167 uses of the word "poor" in the Hebrew Bible that we could delve into. No matter how deeply we choose to dive into individual references in this opening paragraph, at the end of the day, God loves the poor throughout the Hebrew Bible.

Zechariah 7:9-10 (NRSV) [9] Thus says the LORD of hosts: Render true judgments, show kindness and mercy to one another; [10] do not oppress the widow, the orphan, the alien, or the poor; and do not devise evil in your hearts against one another.

Deuteronomy 24:15 (NRSV) ¹⁵ You shall pay them their wages daily before sunset, because they are poor and their livelihood depends on them; otherwise they might cry to the LORD against you, and you would incur guilt.

Psalm 10:2-3 (NRSV) ² In arrogance the wicked persecute the poor— let them be caught in the schemes they have devised. ³ For the wicked boast of the desires of their heart, those greedy for gain curse and renounce the LORD.

Whether God is extolling his people to show kindness to the poor, pay the poor, or stop persecuting the poor, it is clear the poor hold the special attention of God.

In addition to the Hebrew Scriptures, we find 37 uses of the word "poor" in the New Testament. The first words Luke recorded of Jesus' post-baptismal ministry are Isaiah's promise of deliverance for the poor. The story is in Luke 4:16-21 (NRSV)

¹⁶ When [Jesus] came to Nazareth, where he had been brought up, he went to the synagogue on the Sabbath day, as was his custom. He stood up to read, ¹⁷ and the scroll of the prophet Isaiah was given to him. He unrolled the scroll and found the place where it was written:
    ¹⁸ "The Spirit of the Lord is upon me,
        because he has anointed me
            to bring good news to the poor.
He has sent me to proclaim release to the captives
        and recovery of sight to the blind,
            to let the oppressed go free,
    ¹⁹ to proclaim the year of the Lord's favor."
²⁰ And he rolled up the scroll, gave it back to the attendant, and sat down. The eyes of all in the synagogue were fixed on him. ²¹ Then he began to say to them, "Today this scripture has been fulfilled in your hearing."

Through out Jesus' ministry, the words of Isaiah were a road map. He brought Good News, released captives, healed blindness and restored the fortunes of widows. Jesus provided blessings to persons experiencing many types of scarcity of resources. It wasn't just about money, Jesus truly loved the poor.

The wicked and the greedy are synonymized throughout the Bible, as they withhold blessings for personal benefit while allowing the poor to cry out to God for sustenance. God's Word promises to repay this type of selfish unkindness. Redemption, in fact, takes the form of bringing solutions to persons who have insufficient resources in God's bountiful world. God loves to provide blessings to those with insufficient resources. The Good News gets even better. God wants all people to love what God loves. Throughout the Bible, the message is clearly presented: God desires for all people to provide for each other, and specifically for those possessing insufficient resources; the poor, downtrodden, fatherless, widowed, orphaned, and victimized masses. The first step in God's economy is always Love. The process is presented as follows: Love each other, Supply provisions sufficient to generate thanksgiving to God, Enjoy God together. Failure to follow the process is expressed in Scripture as an insult to God. There are many examples of this idea in Scripture, presented here are but a few:

Proverbs 14:31 (NRSV)
[31] Those who oppress the poor insult their Maker,
  but those who are kind to the needy honor him.

Leviticus 19:10 (NRSV)
You shall not strip your vineyard bare, or gather the fallen grapes of your vineyard; you shall leave them for the poor and the alien: I am the Lord your God.

James 2:1-8 (NRSV)

My brothers and sisters, do you with your acts of favoritism really believe in our glorious Lord Jesus Christ? [2] For if a person with gold rings and in fine clothes comes into your assembly, and if a poor person in dirty clothes also comes in, [3] and if you take notice of the one wearing the fine clothes and say, "Have a seat here, please," while to the one who is poor you say, "Stand there," or, "Sit at my feet," [4] have you not made distinctions among yourselves, and become judges with evil thoughts? [5] Listen, my beloved brothers and sisters. Has not God chosen the poor in the world to be rich in faith and to be heirs of the kingdom that he has promised to those who love him? [6] But you have dishonored the poor. Is it not the rich who oppress you? Is it not they who drag you into court? [7] Is it not they who blaspheme the excellent name that was invoked over you? [8] You do well if you really fulfill the royal law according to the scripture, "You shall love your neighbor as yourself."

This is the Good News: people get to love God and their neighbor fully and completely. Love for our neighbor means fully, completely and *equally* if James' message is to be taken at face value. Rich neighbors and poor neighbors, all people get the opportunity to love all persons who are created, according to Genesis 1, in the image of God.

It is important to mention that our poor neighbor is a by-product of cultural advantage. Gustavo Gutiérrez is a noted Christian author and serves as a professor at Notre Dame. He is considered the founder of Liberation Theology. Gutiérrez writes,

"But the poor person does not exist as an inescapable fact of destiny. His or her existence is not politically neutral, and it is not ethically innocent. The poor are a by-product of the system in which we live and for which we are responsible. They are marginalized by our social and cultural world. They are the oppressed, exploited proletariat, robbed of the fruit of their labor and despoiled of their humanity. Hence the poverty of the poor is not a call to generous relief action, but a demand that we go and build a different social order." 3

To follow through on this logic we can say this: if a person benefits from the culture, that person is responsible for the oppression, exploitation and despoiling of the humanity of the poor. This sounds like a harsh reality. It would indeed be very harsh, but for this one amazing truth...*the poor have great wealth to offer the penitent oppressor.*

Poor neighbors, in particular, have had the opportunity to develop some very effective coping strategies which are tremendously helpful to learn. People who have experienced poverty and those who have lived in poverty for generations have excellent survival skills which have been forged in the furnace of scarcity and pain. The wealth of poverty is located in these skills. The poor live the skill of True Reliance, reliance on God and self. When there are no resources to rely on; one learns to do, make do and do without. The poor practice the skill of Imaginative Scheduling when there are multiple part-time jobs and no car. The poor have excellent Networking skills developed by sharing time and trading favors with friends and family. The poor excel in Experiential Strength Development: people learn they are capable of facing adversity, because they have had lots of practice. Tough times are doable because the best predictor of future reality is past performance. Surviving difficult experience teaches the poor better skills with which to confront future issues.

All persons who labor amongst this group of social by-products (the poor) have the opportunity to gain an understanding of God's great deliverance as understood by those who have experienced the reality of needing to be delivered. A harsh reality and a blessing all in one, truly this is the way of the Lord. We have seen it time and again in God's world: Exodus into the Desert, Promised Land battlegrounds, Golgothic salvation...God surely has shown us that sacrifice which becomes blessing is the way to reorder a sin-sickened world order. People in God's world order must

---

3 Courtesy of Yale University: http://www.yale.edu/divinity/fb/Day_37_Gutierrez_excerpts.pdf

battle for peace, work for rest, and give to receive. Ultimately, the joy/ pain of redemptive living amongst the poor begins with time spent among those persons whom people and social systems are least likely to value.

As it turns out, it is quite simple to begin laboring in this field of great bounty. The first thing to do is simply go out and meet the neighbors. Spending time together is the best platform from which to develop true and loving relationships. If society is to learn the wealth of poverty, social activists are going to need to spend the valuable resource of time to mine this wealth. Large scale events and classes are no substitute for sitting down and investing one-on-one time valuing one another. In recent years we have seen an increase in the desire of well meaning persons and organizations to attempt to understand the culture and condition of poverty through "poverty simulations."[4] In a simulation each participant is assigned a role, family and living situation and is asked to assume the role of that persona - whether that is a 9 year old girl or a 75 year old widower. When reading the material prior to the start of the simulation middle class values shine — planning, organizing, hopefulness, assuming everything will go right and things will make sense. However, once the simulation begins it becomes obvious that life in poverty does not follow any culture's rules. No matter what is tried something always seems to go wrong. With no resources to handle the problem, another thing goes wrong, and another, and another like a chain reaction. At the end of a poverty simulation, people often feel powerless, victimized and defeated. Unfortunately, these feelings don't change perceptions over the long term, leaving the nagging myth in place that people in poverty choose to remain poor (ie: fall victim to endless chain reactions of resourcelessness *on purpose*).

One problem that can cause chain reactions within poor communities involves access to reliable transportation. To begin investing time in poverty stricken neighbors one might take this into account in real life rather than remaining safely in a simulation. By travelling to the neighbor's home

---

4 Among the poverty simulations that we have had good experience with is the Missouri Association for Community Action Simulation. (www.communityaction.org/Poverty%20 Simulation.aspx)

or choosing meeting locations that capitalize on public transportation systems some challenging chain reactions might be avoided by those already battling for resources. Certainly meeting in the homes of those persons who are living out the struggles inherent with poverty is the best way to see first-hand the lessons which can be learned in these environs. Meet the neighbors at work, church or the grocery store, share a cool drink, and talk about the stuff of life. See, that wasn't very hard, was it?

When these relationships begin to develop, it is imperative to hear the stories of the poor with a compassionate and inquisitive ear. What strengths does this story reveal? What needs are present in the conversation? How is this reality keeping bondage at the forefront and the wealth of God in chains? The temptation is to swoop in with answers to problems as defined by the affluent and powerful culture of the day. Sadly, these rescue efforts can never be successful. People who are gripped by poverty have no hope for the future and, therefore, have no way to set goals to reach that future. Poverty diminishes people. Handing out money may solve a particular problem at a particular moment in time, but it will not heal the tunnel vision that becomes reality when resources are scarce. "Scarcity captures the mind," writes Mullainathan and Shafir in an as yet unpublished new book.[5] In a review on this book, Oliver Burkeman for The Guardian notes,

> "[Scarcity] promotes tunnel vision, helping us focus on the crisis at hand but making us "less insightful, less forward-thinking, less controlled". Wise long-term decisions and willpower require cognitive resources. Poverty leaves far less of those resources at our disposal. Merely asking poorer people to contemplate a hypothetical £1,000 car repair, one study by the authors shows, impairs their performance on intelligence tests as much as missing a night's sleep – about 13 or 14 IQ points."[6]

5 http://www.theguardian.com/books/2013/aug/23/scarcity-sendhil-mullainathan-eldar-shafir?CMP=twt_fd
6 IBID

As cognitive resources become scarce, narrative resources become the primary mode through which the wealth of poverty becomes translated. These narrative accounts must be mined for their valuable information, but they cannot be mined until they are heard. Listen to the stories of the poor. The value of these narratives is so profound that each chapter in this book will be built in and on these narrative accounts and an appendix of collected stories will be included at the end of this book. The stories will be told here as an instructive on how to listen, because listening through the narrative is the surest way to immerse privileged understandings fully enough to grasp the wealth of poverty.

Listening to the stories offers greater opportunity in listening for gift-edness as well. When people's lives get full of details like feeding kids, getting an affordable transmission for the broken car in the front yard, meeting with probation/parole officers, waiting for hours at government offices, helping evicted friends move while the police look on; it becomes difficult to see talents and abilities as gifts of God designed to edify the Kingdom. To mine the wealth of giftedness in participants from the culture of poverty, listening carefully to the narratives becomes central to the recognition of giftedness. As soon as gifts and graces are recognized, they must also be affirmed, affirmed again, and over-affirmed. Persons bound by poverty see value in everyone they know, except themselves. One consequence of a scarcity of resources is strong and gifted individuals place themselves last in line to receive resources. This heroic gesture results in self-esteem issues wherein the strongest and most capable feel as though they are the least deserving. These self-esteem issues are often thinly veiled in bravado and arrogance. It has been called the "I am the piece of trash around which the whole world revolves" syndrome. The weight of feeling useless, while knowing the survival of the family is one's sole responsibility, warps a person's ability to account their own gifted-ness as valuable. The giftedness of these heroic individuals is a reservoir of great value just waiting to be recognized, realized and capitalized in the Kingdom of God.

As gifts are affirmed, leadership must also be affirmed. Inviting new and untested leaders is one of those things the Kingdom of God is famous for doing badly. There is so much fear around safety within the sanctuary opportunities are missed in provision of sanctuary to those developing newly identified leadership gifts. To begin cultivating new leaders from the culture of poverty, first let go of preconceived notions about leadership requirements. People who have been raised in different cultures will have different gifts, different styles, different values and different mannerisms. It would be improper to expect these persons to behave as though they were raised in middle-class America. The hidden rules and understandings ingrained in the privileged are quite different than the hidden rules and understandings learned in poverty and generational poverty. Success across this cultural boundary will require creating systems where folks can lead something with a safety net first, without managing the process, just pointing toward the goal and being willing to be surprised. Trial runs at leadership where the current power holder acts as safety net/consultant/cheerleader will empower new leaders to act independently in small things as confidence is built toward the goal of leading ever larger projects.

God loves the poor. People can invest time and listening and attentiveness and leadership training to great advantage for the poor. But, why? Why would a privileged member of the culture choose to invest in those whom God loves? In 2 Corinthians 9:11-12, Paul discusses an offering for the poor in Jerusalem and promises this benefit to sharing with the poor. "You will be enriched in every way for your great generosity, which will produce thanksgiving to God through us; for the rendering of this ministry not only supplies the needs of the saints but also overflows with many thanksgivings to God." Loving the poor, the destitute, the widowed, or the victimized fully and completely is a gift from God for the culturally advantaged. Loving the poor is a gift crafted especially for those who gain safety and security from the same social structures that break and impoverish others. Spending time with the poor is also pivotal to mining the wealth of those whom God favors. Time is the most precious resource a mortal being has. How we spend or invest our time is one of our greatest decisions. We actually create value in and for the Kingdom of God by capitalizing the strengths of the poor. As was noted earlier in this chapter, listening is paramount to practicing this value added ministry of presence. Begin listening for the values of the community in the stories of the target community. Begin listening for the gifts that are hidden in the counter-culture poverty generates. Begin listening through the static of a life lived in a different culture. Listening uncovers a treasure trove of gifts and graces in persons and communities. Through these gifts and graces, Christian community can be designed outside the boxes of expectation that the power culture has taught is proper. Cross-cultural processes and sensitivities will aid in creating Kingdom of God value through the incorporation and combination of the strengths generated by each culture.

To operate effectively in a cross-cultural reality, it is generally helpful to understand the broad strokes of the other (not your own) culture. The next chapter will expose one definition of culture along with some of the most common tripping points when disciples attempt interacting with the culture of poverty.

Not-So-Simple Wondering

1. God loves the poor. What other passages spring to mind that show how God loves the poor, in both the Old and New Testaments? Why does God love the poor?

2. God expects Christ-followers to love the poor. What other passages in the Old and New Testament would highlight God's desire for his followers to love the poor? Why does God want his followers to love the poor?

3. Name the barriers that could prevent you or your group from loving the poor. What would it take to remove or mitigate these barriers? What kind of commitment would it take?

4. What gifts do the poor bring to the table? What abilities and skills have they developed that are not in you or your group's normal skill set?

CHAPTER 2

A Cohesive and Identifiable Culture

In the year preceding their marriage, Andrew asked Melissa to help with aquarium maintenance. Andrew had a perfectly balanced aquarium. He had put in exacting amounts/types of bottom substrates (like gravel, rocks, hidey holes, etc). He installed the proper filtration. He made sure to get the right types and numbers of fish to support one another's good and bad habits. He had selected and planted the perfect plants to support his ecosystem requirements for cleaning and aeration. His lights did the perfect amount of warming to aid the evaporation cycle necessary for proper salinization. He kept the temperature in the proper range to maintain all the life process of the water and the inhabitants that occupied the water. He added only the correct food and plant fertilizer to maintain a healthy environment inside the tank. The first day of her aquarium responsibilities, Melissa noticed the water had evaporated down about two inches. She added some tap water to keep the water level constant and then went to work.

By the time Andrew arrived home from work, one fish had already died. The water the fish were swimming in was no longer sufficiently balanced to support that fish's comfort level, lifestyle or physical needs. Some of the fish adapted. At least one of the fish could not make the changes necessary for survival. Adaptation became necessary to ensure survival in Andrew's no longer perfect aquarium.

—From the files of Melissa Muzny, Midland, TX

Culture is the water in the aquarium of every person's life. Culture is the organizational environment within which people operate together. Culture includes perfectly balanced sets of rules and behavioral expectations. Cultural capital is the currency used to operate successfully within particular cultural environments. More than just money, cultural capital includes relationships, networks of influence such as group membership, knowledge, skills, education, language, the ability to earn resources *and* money. Extended deprivation of cultural capital results in a culture of poverty marked by its own perfectly balanced values, rules and expected behaviors. Consider it this way: the culture of advantage has added tap water to the aquarium within which the poor are living. The water (culture) no longer provides the tools necessary for survival within the aquarium of poverty. The poor develop survival skills for living in the tainted water. These survival skills, necessary to maintain existence, become part and parcel, a water filtration system that results in survivable conditions, ie: a new culture. This newly created system of imbricated values, rules and expectations (culture) is a strength that can be recognized, identified and capitalized in the Kingdom of God.

Culture is difficult to define. Understanding culture is one part art, one part science, one part observation, one part personal bias, one part self-realization, one part clarification and one part confusion. It is difficult to define the water we are swimming in. It is even more difficult to view the water in another aquarium without swimming in it, which might be a less than survivable possibility. Many social scientists strongly oppose identifying a culture of poverty as, some argue, this creates separations between groups of people that are unnecessary. This book operates from the assumption that identifying differences in the real world is helpful for communicating effectively across those differences. Some will disagree with this assumption. That is OK.

Cultures organize people in a hierarchy of levels based on different dimensions of cultural capital and access to cultural capital. Within a particular culture one will know the rules regarding Language, Religion, Education, Food, Clothing, Parenting Style, Sports and Recreation, Civic Organization and Responsibility, Transportation, Economic Location, World View, and Creative Arts (art, music, entertainment, etc). Each hierarchical level requires behaviors, mores and values in order to operate successfully at that level.

The people who participate in a culture will feel a certain level of comfort with the way things are. The rules of the culture are ingrained below the individual and collective radar of the participants and have evolved over time to become the status quo even when the participants no longer remember why the hierarchy was established. Consider the following story:

A commercial production company hired an expert to come and look at their systems. Their costs for production had sky-rocketed and they couldn't pin point the problem. They knew that their chemicals costs had increased. They understood which process was involved and they were assuming the error was the chemistry in that process. They hired a chemical engineering expert to look into the problem.

After three days of reviewing the process, the expert couldn't see the issue either. Instead of continuing to review the technical specs, she decided to wander around the plant and ask questions. As she moved through the plant she noticed graffiti inside the plant — unusual given the high level of security that it took to get into the plant. She was surprised by the workers general discomfort and unwillingness to talk. Walking through one of the buildings, the building where most of the chemicals were used, she noticed workers cutting the bottoms off of the doors that led from room to room. She stopped and asked what they were doing. They replied by saying they were cutting the bottom of the doors off. She smiled and said, "yes, I can see that, but why are you doing that?" The responded that they needed to do that so when it flooded in the building they could still move from room to room.

Being unaware of any unusual hydrogeologic conditions that would cause frequent flooding she asked the obvious clarifying question, "you mean when it rains too much and the rain floods in the building you need to be able to move from room to room?" "No," the workers answered, "it's so when the tank overflows and floods everything we can move from room to room." She was stunned. They had just told her that costly chemicals from the production line were overflowing their mixing chamber and flooding the building. But none of the operator records indicated this kind of event. The flooding would account for the mysterious rise in chemical costs. She decided to spend some time touring the plant and stayed through every shift to talk to every one of the workers for two nights in a row. She asked questions about their families about what they liked about their work. On the second night they invited her to go out into the grounds of the plant to look for rare mushrooms that grew on the plant grounds. The tank operators were leaving their posts to go out into the grounds and pick the mushrooms. When they got back to their posts they were pulling chemistry samples and posting the results — by then the results looked normal because the tanks had overflowed.

The plant didn't have a chemistry problem. It had an employee relations problem. Apparently a labor dispute from years earlier had ended poorly and the management had become more unyielding in handling their employees. Since the maintenance personnel thought nothing of responding to a request to remove the bottoms of all the doors, we understand that knowledge of the flooding problem was widespread and we also understand that many workers chose to work around the problem rather than dealing with it. The flooding had become a normal part of operations. It meant that communication between departments was rare. It meant that everyone was looking to get their personal job done without caring for the overall health of the system and that no one was putting two and two and two together between the flooding, the mushroom picking, an old smoldering employee dispute, and the loss of profitability through overuse of chemicals. All of these issues were present in the culture of the workers yet not completely visible in the culture of management. The engineer quietly recommended that the plant open the grounds to employees and their families to allow them to gather mushrooms so it wouldn't need to be done during a worker's shift.

Culture clashes like this happen frequently when churches get involved in missions of mercy — giving aid to the immediate need — without understanding the difference between the culture of justice and the culture of mercy. Mercy feeds the hungry one bowl of rice at a time. Justice asks, "What can I give up to create a system where everyone can eat?" Mercy cuts the doors off so that people can move from room to room when things flood. Justice asks why the flood is happening and how it can be stopped.

—Pastor Tina Carter, Parker Lane UMC, Austin, TX

Cultural rules are obvious to the population which successfully operates within a particular aquarium, even rules that don't make any sense, like cutting off the bottoms of the doors. Oftentimes no one has had any reason to question the status quo. Therefore, as a general rule, it is only when participants from other cultures encounter one another that the rules within the hierarchy become questionable. Kingdom of God operations with the poor require the ability to operate successfully within an organized and identifiable culture which may be unknown, unfamiliar or uncomfortable for the cross-cultural operator.

According to some social scientists and educators, poverty instills values and behaviors which are different than those values and behaviors characteristic of middle class culture.[7] Cultural norms in generational poverty are based on survival, relationships, entertainment, and a local world-view. Middle class culture is marked by strong values around work, achievement, security/life-management, and a national world-view. As you can imagine, a person who would sacrifice relationships

---

7 For further reading on American economic cultures see: Small M.L., Harding D.J., Lamont M. (2010). *Reconsidering culture and poverty*. Annals of the American Academy of Political and Social Science 629 (1): 6–27. Ehlig, B., & Payne, R. K. (1999). *What every church member should know about poverty*. Highlands, TX:aha! Process.

for achievement, or vice versa, could run afoul of the culture they intend to work within. Persons who try to pull themselves out of poverty (and into the middle class) struggle mightily when encountering these kinds of limiting factors. Persons in the middle class who attempt to "help" those in poverty struggle mightily to gain the trust of persons who have been victimized by persons or institutions in the power structure.

Persons operating within the culture of poverty have many gifts and talents that rarely look like behaviors that are valued in other cultures. Emotive, expressive language encapsulated in short phrases with poor grammar and limited vocabulary is not generally identified as valuable. Operational capacity within various environs is exceedingly valuable to excel in the culture of poverty. Those who are impoverished must be able to navigate government offices, a different job site every day, a job with many languages spoken but none of them your own, a home without central heat and air, a violent home, no home, a bail bonds office, a crack house, a prison, and a school from another culture. These environs are not generally held as valuable in the culture of power; therefore, the ability to traverse them is not given value either. Creativity and flexibility are the necessary skills underpinning all these capacities, but because the grammar of the community is assessed as "bad," or because the environs within which the operational capacities were learned are proclaimed as negative environs, the creativity and flexibility often go unnoticed. Judging the environment rather than treasuring the beauty that environment has imparted to the persons within it can inadvertently drive a wedge between persons of differing cultures.

To begin the journey of separating person from culture, and skill set from the environment within which that skill was gained, the participants from the culture of power must set aside judgments based in the values of power culture and begin ferreting out these valuable underpins within the culture of poverty. What is important in this situation? Why is it important? Are they cutting off the bottom of the doors or is there a

Harrington, Michael (1962). *The Other America: Poverty in the United States.* Simon & Schuster.

contemporary or important reason for this behavior? This questioning of the values of the power culture will be more difficult for the middle class as maintaining the status quo is important to maintaining status within the middle class experience. Whereas the rich can dress in poor clothes and walk around for an afternoon before returning to the family castle, the middle class culture can be diluted by opening itself to the values of another culture which has been judged as less valuable. There is inherent in the middle class experience an *upward* mobility and any idea that suggests moving *downward* in Class strata can be counted as a threat. Still, cross-cultural encounters require meeting the target culture on its own ground and according to its own values. American history certainly bears this out in the woefully inadequate treatment of the Native American and African American cultures. The hope of the authors is that history will not need to repeat itself again in contemporary cross-cultural treatment of the poor. In order to capitalize the wealth of poverty, the culture of power must learn to operate effectively in a culture which organizes and expresses value and knowledge in ways which are not only different, but that may also create discomfort for those who have benefitted from the culture of power. Some cultural realities that present the greatest limiting opportunities for those working in cultures marked by scarcity are time, acceptance, toleration of difficult circumstances, survival skills, unjust systems, and an understanding of need. The successive chapters will explicate each of these cultural realities and the motives, values and strengths that can be found underpinning that reality.

Not-so-simple Wondering

1. Imagine going to a party with people like you. You are hanging out, having a good time. Now imagine a person from a culture of poverty entering the room. How would you know they were different? What unspoken rules would they be unaware of? List as many as you can.

2. Now imagine you are attending a party with people from the next culture level up. You are nervous and anxious to prove that you belong. How might they discover you were different? What unspoken rules might you break? List as many as you can.

3. Reflecting back, was it easier to identify the person who "didn't belong" or to imagine rules you don't know? How difficult would it be for a person to change the culture they swim in?

4. Do you identify more with the culture of poverty or the culture of power? Name the barriers that limit your ability to understand the other culture.

CHAPTER 3

The Wealth of Imaginative Scheduling

"Ellen" grew up with no stability in a single parent home. By the time she was a young woman she had three children by three different men. By the early 90's she was in and out of trouble with the law. She spent some time in jail in 1991-1993. When Child Protective Services (CPS) removed her children from her home due to neglect in the early 2000's she lost everything she had to live for and dove headlong into drug use. In 2004 the State took action against Ellen, forcing her to pay child support to the state for the children that the state had in foster care. In 2005 she was convicted of multiple drug charges and incarcerated. While she was incarcerated the child support payments accrued. In 2011 Ellen was paroled to Austin, TX (far from her home town). She was paroled to Austin because she had no previous address to be paroled to and there were vacancies in halfway houses in Austin. Ellen made a decision to change her life.

By 2012 Ellen committed her life to Jesus, started attending church, found regular employment (at 8.50 an hour) and started to rebuild her life. Finding herself paroled far from home she was also far from the influences and patterns of her old life. It looked like she would be able to turn her life around. Then she got a summons from the court in her home town. The Attorney General was requesting Ellen be put on probation or incarcerated for failure to pay support from 2005-2011 while she was incarcerated. In order to avoid being jailed for contempt, Ellen had to take off work, find a way to travel 250 miles to appear in court for the purpose of scheduling a real court date—one which Ellen will have to take time off and travel for as well.

Going to court is scary even if you have many resources. It's terrifying if you don't have money, have very little sobriety, and don't have a lot of academic skill. Court in real life doesn't look like court on television. There is a dress code in most court rooms. The dress code can vary from county to county and court to court. There is a behavior code as well—also highly variable. Ellen will have to wade through the hidden rules of the court in order to make an arrangement with the court to pay the more than $25,000 in child support and fines that accrued during her incarceration."

—Excerpted from Its About Relationships: Images of Ministry.

On the fourth day, according to Genesis 1:14-19, God set the sun and moon in the sky to govern the times and the seasons, the days and the years. In the modern era, time is a hard taskmaster. Time is unforgiving to all things under her tyranny. The poor have developed strategies and capacities to survive this unforgiving task master, to make the best of the few years humans are allowed to live upon this earth. The poor can manage time whether there is a lot of it, such as would occur during a period of unemployment, or a very little, owing to the busy-ness required for survival.

The poor live day by day and "in the moment." Scarcity teaches that no one knows what will happen today, tomorrow, or next week. There is no controlling what comes next in the march of time. The only set of controllables is found in responding to events as they occur. When an individual is focused on survival, and the pressing needs of the day require immediate decisions and actions, people cannot get out of crisis mode. This reality limits the impoverished to an existence without a future tense.

Life without a future expends all its resources right now. There is nothing for which to save and no consequences more serious than the present struggle. There is a reduced willingness to delay gratification and an unexplainable preference for short-term gains, at the cost of larger long-term benefits, when people are unmoored from the self they will become in the future.[8] This freedom from the bonds of tomorrow makes the poor a force to be reckoned with.

Imagine a single mom with 3 kids under the age of 12. They go to school during the day and she is able to work. She has to take public transportation, but she is saving up for a car. One of her kids gets sick. Now she has to take off from work, losing the day's wages, pay for their transportation to the doctor, pay for the exam, pay for the medicine, pay for a trip to the pharmacy, and get them home. Three days later, the other two kids come down with the same thing and she is starting to feel bad too. Would anyone in this situation continue to save for a car? Or would they get medicine for their kids? The resources must be spent now to overcome the struggles of the now. There is no sense of future, only an ongoing crisis and struggle rhythm.

Poverty also alters the community's view of the past. Memory can be a dangerous neighborhood. Neglect, child abuse and sexual abuse of children and adolescents are prevalent throughout modern society, even in neighborhoods with scarce resources. Trauma caused by witnessing violent events is extremely common in poorer communities, as well. Any form of child abuse and many other forms of trauma are known to cause severe psychological and emotional consequences. It is also common for traumatized people to make deliberate efforts to avoid thoughts or feelings about the traumatic event and to avoid activities or situations which may remind them of the event. Families without resources have greater difficulty obtaining care for the inherent psychiatric and dissociative disorders that arise from such abuse. Conversations about past traumatic events are

---

8 For a deeper understanding of self/future self relationships consider: Ersner-Hershfield, H., Garton, M. T., Ballard, K., Samanez-Larkin, G. R., & Knutson, B. (2009). Don't stop thinking about tomorrow: Individual differences in future self-continuity account for saving.

genuinely difficult to start, and without professional intervention, these conversations are of little healing value. It often becomes easier to eliminate thoughts of the past than to confront traumatic memory.

Poor communities are built between a troubling past and an unforeseeable future expending all energies in the moment, for the moment. Many of these moments are filled with crises. Sleep schedules suffered last night due to a loud party at the crack house down the block. No one had time or money for laundry, so two kids are going commando for the day. Aunt Margo's car didn't start, and the last bus to be on time to work already passed through the neighborhood. Payday is two days away and all that's left in the cupboard is dry cereal. Maybe there'll be time to sell plasma today to get some food money which will take less time than going down to the food stamp office. Riding the bus will mean arriving late to work, making the paycheck short, compounded by the fact that there are still medical bills to pay on from the emergency room trip last year. Getting to job #2 is harder and Aunt Margo isn't going to have the car for several days while one of her mechanic friends tries to find time to get it fixed. There's no money to cover the check for a new bus pass so another $35 overdraft fee will be added if that check hits before Friday. Too much drama already today, no more decision making, except that Nathan down the street just called, the police are there evicting them. Can they stay on the couch for a couple days?

Living in the moment makes it possible for impoverished families to negotiate the myriad issues that arise simply from being impoverished. Cars are generally cheaper and older which results in more breakdowns and necessitates more maintenance. Poorer neighborhoods are often places of violence and emotional dissonance as it is wretchedly frustrating to be powerless in so many ways. Multiple part-time jobs are harder to juggle than one full-time job. Errands are exponentially more difficult using public transportation or public assistance which is scheduled according to the needs of the government rather than the needs of the individual. Poverty requires Imaginative Scheduling and a learned patience to navigate the crises and agencies that make survival possible.

People outside the culture of poverty have other resources they can rely on so they can avoid the skill of Imaginative Scheduling. The mom that has to get her kids to soccer practice generally has a reliable SUV. While the children are at practice, she can run on errand, check her e-mail, or build her social network with the other parents. Next week, if one of the kids needs a ride from school, she can probably ask one of the other parents. Reliable transportation, economic resources, and an understanding of social norms, insulate her and her family from the Imaginative Scheduling associated with "in-the-moment" crisis management.

Living in the moment can also result in spiraling repercussions that contribute to the cycle of generational poverty. Anything on a regular schedule can present difficulties for the family lacking reliable transportation, limited access to health care, and rotating or overnight work schedules. One in ten kindergarten students in poverty miss a month or more of school every year. Missing 10% of one year's school days is defined as chronic absence. Those who miss 10 percent of the year in kindergarten perform poorly in 1st grade, and, for low-income children, poor performance persists through 5th grade. As these children reach high school age, chronic absence is a key factor in predicting a propensity to drop out.[9] The same can be seen in the adult environment. Missing work or being late for work often has repercussions. If you are late a certain number of times, you can be fired. If you miss a certain number of days, you can be fired. Being at the doctor with a sick child at the end of the month generally means the prepaid cell phone minutes are all used up. No way to call work, no way to make the line move more quickly produces a no call/no show, again, grounds for termination.

Another scheduled reality that presents limiting factors to persons in poverty is the working environment with its hidden rules based on middle class cultural norms. Timeliness and attendance are only the beginning of

9 More research on absence issues in poverty can be found at: http://www.spotlightonpoverty.org/ OutOfTheSpotlight.aspx?id=f88fb451-91bc-4ae2-9e65-c566dc9f0806

the difficulties set forward in the working environment. There are several ways the middle class maintains the status quo: including managing a rule set that insulates the wealthy from the lower classes and remaining heavily invested in the political, religious, social, and economic system from which the middle class derives benefit.[10] How one sits, eats, looks, walks, communicates and all manner of other outward indicators illustrates whether one is "in" or "out." Once identified as "out," one loses access to promotability and gains access to a host of disciplinary options that serve to continually remind the impoverished to remain in their place. Imagine how it feels to be employed in three part-time jobs, raising two of your brother's children while he serves in Afghanistan and being told: "If you would only pull yourself up by your boot straps and show some initiative we wouldn't have to write you up again." Use of the parent voice to cow subordinates is a key middle class cultural indicator in the workplace.

There are at least three voices that bear on this conversation; adult, parent, and child. The child voice is characterized by whining, defensiveness, victimization, non-verbal cues and strong negativity as well as being playful, spontaneous and curious. The Parent voice is authoritative, directive, evaluative, demanding and sometimes punitive or threatening as well as holding the possibility for being loving and supportive. The Adult voice is non-judgmental, factual and often presents in questions with an attitude of win-win. The chart that follows illustrates these three voices.[11]

---

10 Weber, Max, The Protestant Ethic and the Spirit of Capitalism, London: Allen & Unwin, 1930.
11 Excerpted from A Framework for Understanding Poverty Workbook by Ruby K. Payne © 2012 aha! Process. Permission to reprint.

Child	Parent	Adult
Quit picking on me.	You shouldn't (should) do that.	In what ways could this be resolved?
You don't love me.	It's wrong (right) to do _____.	What factors will determine the effectiveness of …?
You want me to leave.	That's stupid, immature, out of line, ridiculous.	I would like to recommend:
Nobody likes (loves) me.	Life's not fair. Get busy.	What are choices in this situation?
I hate you.	You are good, bad, worthless, beautiful.	I am comfortable (uncomfortable) with:
You're ugly.	Any judgmental, evaluative comment.	Options that could be considered are:
You make me sick.	You do as I say.	To be comfortable, I need the following things to occur:
It's your fault.	If you weren't so _____, this wouldn't happen to you.	These are the consequences of that choice/action:
Don't blame me.	Why can't you be like _____?	We agree to disagree.
She, he, _____ did it.		
You make me mad.		Note. Adapted from the work of Eric Berne, 1996.

Excerpted from A Framework for Understanding Poverty Workbook by Ruby K. Payne © 2012 aha! Process. Permission to reprint.

The Adult voice is most certainly the voice of Executive and Political Leadership. The Parental voice is generally the voice of Mid-level Management and the middle class. The Child voice is most often the sound of the disempowered. Keeping in mind that the definitions as listed here were written by educators in the middle class trying to understand and define the culture of poverty, the value of understanding ways organized cultures create and recognize outcasts is gained.

For some poor workers, battling for their very survival against a scarcity of resources, being addressed by the adult voice feels like disrespect. For the mid-level manager, Imaginative Scheduling, when it looks like several minutes late everyday, feels like disrespect. When the pressures of their lives drive these two into a confrontation, the one least likely to keep their job is the person from the culture of poverty. Malcolm Gladwell, author of "The Tipping Point," claims that success is determined by the 10,000 hour rule noting that Bill Gates, The Beatles and Mozart among others, all required 10 years of practice (equivalent to 10,000 hours).[12] "Genius is a function of hours put in and not personal gifts" and 10,000 hours of practice is the magic number to achieve greatness.[13] When persons from the culture of poverty leave or lose their jobs the opportunity to meet the 10,000 rule diminishes exponentially.

Imaginative scheduling is necessary for persons in poverty because it takes longer to do almost everything when resources are scarce. People are more dependent on one another, and on whatever item they are waiting for, than on the hands of a clock. There are no guarantees that the bus will be on time or that the lines at a government office will move quickly enough. In addition to processes taking longer, there is a need to take advantage of whatever possibilities arise for entertainment and escape — the only things which make this incredibly difficult life more tolerable. Addiction issues arise under the escape category as no human being can survive abject hopelessness long term. More frequently, though, escape looks like gathering with one's family, whether blood or collected family, and hanging out, watching TV, playing music or making not-so-deep-nor-meaningful conversation, and allowing the cares of the world to melt away for a very short time.

Learning this level of flexibility and imagination in scheduling can help the middle and upper classes begin to think of their communities in terms of organic wholeness. Relationships become the most important

12 Malcolm Gladwell (2008), Outliers: The Story of Success, Little, Brown and Company.
13 IBID

goal across class strata. Control takes a back seat to loving people. Life no longer has to revolve around self, immediate family, and the hands of a clock. Imaginative Scheduling allows the freedom of living in the moment without fear of the future and without being imprisoned by traditions past. Imaginative Scheduling presents more opportunities to live out the words of Matthew 6:31-34:

> 31 Therefore do not worry, saying, 'What will we eat?' or 'What will we drink?' or 'What will we wear?' 32 For it is the Gentiles who strive for all these things; and indeed your heavenly Father knows that you need all these things. 33 But strive first for the kingdom of God and his righteousness, and all these things will be given to you as well. 34 "So do not worry about tomorrow, for tomorrow will bring worries of its own. Today's trouble is enough for today.

Believing that God has given us time to mark the seasons and the years can give us the impetus to start acting out New Testament Christianity just the way Jesus preached it in His Sermons on the Mount. The Lord's Prayer also limits us to the one day at a time focus saying, "Give us this day our daily bread." Imaginative Scheduling is the way of the kingdom of God and the culture of poverty is a great place to learn it.

This book is not the first place Christians have tried to communicate to other Christians on the topic of living in the now. Please find below the daily meditation penned and utilized by Pope John XXIII.

1. Only for today, I will seek to live the livelong day positively without wishing to solve the problems of my life all at once.

2. Only for today, I will take the greatest care of my appearance: I will dress modestly; I will not raise my voice; I will be courteous in my behaviour; I will not criticize anyone; I will not claim to improve or to discipline anyone except myself.

3. Only for today, I will be happy in the certainty that I was created to be happy, not only in the other world but also in this one.

4. Only for today, I will adapt to circumstances, without requiring all circumstances to be adapted to my own wishes.

5. Only for today, I will devote 10 minutes of my time to some good reading, remembering that just as food is necessary to the life of the body, so good reading is necessary to the life of the soul.

6. Only for today, I will do one good deed and not tell anyone about it.

7. Only for today, I will do at least one thing I do not like doing; and if my feelings are hurt, I will make sure that no one notices.

8. Only for today, I will make a plan for myself: I may not follow it to the letter, but I will make it. And I will be on guard against two evils: hastiness and indecision.

9. Only for today, I will firmly believe, despite appearances, that the good Providence of God cares for me as no one else who exists in this world.

10. Only for today, I will have no fears. In particular, I will not be afraid to enjoy what is beautiful and to believe in goodness. Indeed, for 12 hours I can certainly do what might cause me consternation were I to believe I had to do it all my life

Pope John XXIII's Daily Decalogue is a fine meditation to help needy humans focus their attentions on one other and on sharing the things of God. That would be Imaginative Scheduling at its finest.

Not-So-Simple Wondering

1. What is Imaginative Scheduling? Why is it so important to survival for the poor? What benefits or lessons could be learned from Imaginative Scheduling?

2. If you want to reach out to the poor, how does understanding Imaginative Scheduling influence your decisions? Where should you meet? Is there transportation/child care? What do you do when they are 'late'? What crisis will be going on as you talk?

3. How would your life benefit from the skill of Imaginative Scheduling? What benefit could you or your group derive from living in the moment? What is preventing you from living in the moment? Where is the rhythmic process of God's times and seasons in your daily experience? Where is that rhythmic process truncated by applying resources that insulate you from the pain of living?

CHAPTER 4

The Wealth of Experiential Strength Development

On the eve of Easter, the girls gathered up the sheets and towels and began the joyful tradition of fashioning Easter nests. The Easter Bunny will only bring presents if the nest is properly colorful and filled with enticing candies. This Easter Eve, Dad has gone missing again. Surely he'll be home soon. Sadly, he doesn't make it home until well after bedtime. Sadly, he is also really drunk. He is in the bedroom screaming at Mom about some perceived infidelity. Apparently he has proof this time, proof in his jacket pocket. Where is that jacket? Oh yes, it is on the chair in the girls' bedroom, which also happens to be the living room as the conditions are a bit crowded. As he careens through the house, he trips over and scatters the nest of the eldest daughter. She is so frail already. She doesn't need this kind of bad news. Her little sister gets up as Dad makes his way back to his room to show Mom his "evidence." The nest is put right very quietly so as to avoid attracting Dad's attention when he's in such a foul mood. While the younger girl crouches over the nest, she notices that the door to the adult's room is ajar. She catches a glimpse of him now, strangling her mother, shaking her like a rag doll. Somehow she can't help herself, she jumps to her feet and bull rushes her Father, her only thought is that someone needs to stop this. Daddy catches this little girl mid-tackle and flings her across the room, dropping Mom and whirling around for the follow-up that will most assuredly be exponentially worse due to the disrespect shown by such a stupid child. The blows come quickly as she struggles to move away, but, finally he gets a good strong hold on the back of her neck and is able to lift her straight off the floor. The great roundhouse punch catches her jaw just below the ear as she flies from his grip and into the half closed door. The door crashes off its hinges and onto the floor. As the crumpled little girl slides blissfully into unconsciousness, the last thing she sees in the blood trickling out of her Mother's ear. She sleeps, hoping it was enough. When she comes to the next morning, she immediately realizes that it wasn't enough. The Easter Bunny never visited the nests, never left presents, and she was never enough again.

— From *Stories of the Congregational Wesleyan Church,* 2009

From a home such as this, what could the grown up child have to offer? The way she handles stress will be radically different from the 'norm'. The way she responds to crisis will come from a place of survivability. However, her loyalty, though perhaps given to the wrong people, will be incredibly strong. Her instincts are to fight, not flight. These attributes, though formed differently, can be a source of wealth for the girl trying to crawl her way out of poverty. The middle class managers she will encounter can choose whether to lift her up by recognizing and capitalizing her strengths, or they can ensure that she continues to crawl beneath the hidden rules that maintain the status quo.

Capitalizing the wealth of poverty can be envisioned through practices of Positive Psychology. Positive Psychology is a field of human development which claims the belief that people want to lead meaningful lives with fulfilling experiences in all aspects of life. Martin Seligman, father of positive psychology, and co-author, Mihaly Csikszentmihalyi, wrote; "We believe that a psychology of positive human functioning will arise, which achieves a scientific understanding and effective interventions to build thriving individuals, families, and communities."[14] The middle class philosophy that the poor person is simply lazy or undetermined would have no place in positive psychology. Positive approaches are based in the belief that persons who are operating from their strengths will be more effective and happier and suffer less dis-ease in the course of a lifetime. Focusing on the weakness or sickness of an individual often reinforces that sickness or weakness and may also add a destructive edge of low self-esteem.

Building upon people's strengths rather than continually harping on their differences can yield tremendous harvest for the kingdom of God and in God's local organization, generally called the church. The strengths that are instilled through experiences of the culture of poverty include, but are not limited to: 1) Loyalty, 2) Courage, 3) Resilience, 4) Adaptability, 5) Patience and 6) Tolerance. Each of these strengths needs to be clearly understood in order to make the most of the capital it brings to each and every reader. Following is a framework for understanding these strengths.

Loyalty is a state of being which is marked by devotion and affection. Loyalty has been learned through experiences which required dependence on another. These experiences of interdependence go far deeper than borrowing a cup of sugar. These life transforming experiences are the times friends walk home together in the middle night so neither gets raped, murdered or sold into human slavery rings. Loyalty is forged in the furnace of humans behaving salvifically through the day to day grinding which poverty dishes out. Loyalty is earned when one person or family faced with a world of "I cant's" experiences a single person or family that offers some hope or possibility of escape or even just survivability. Loyalty cannot be earned in an afternoon or in the gift of a happy meal drive-by delivered to a pan-handler at the red light. Loyalty is earned by being present in time

---

14 Seligman, Martin E.P.; Csikszentmihalyi, Mihaly (2000). "Positive Psychology: An Introduction". American Psychologist 55 (1): 5–14.

and space and participating in life together. Here are some suggestions that may help capitalize this gift for the kingdom of God:

- ✓ Be present. Come early and stay late.
- ✓ Walk the neighborhood.
- ✓ Recognize accomplishments.
- ✓ Smile often and look people in the eye.
- ✓ Give more than what is required and ask others to meet your needs as well.

Loyalty, once earned, will yield countless returns. Persons who are loyal will bear the burdens of life together, protecting one another, and building self-esteem through unyielding acceptance. In addition, the book of Proverbs tells us loyalty and faithfulness find favor with God. Proverbs 3:3-4, "Do not let loyalty and faithfulness forsake you; bind them around your neck, write them on the tablet of your heart. So you will find favor and good repute in the sight of God and of people." Loyalty is an excellent gift which is found in abundance in the culture of poverty.

Courage is the capacity to behave rightly when it is risky to do so. An oft quoted reference from Oliver Wendell Holmes goes like this, "Courage is about doing what you're afraid to do. There can be no courage unless you're scared." Courage is an absolute requirement in the cauldron of community violence, domestic violence, addiction, single parenting, workplaces with hidden rules, and payday loan/pawn shops looking to take your future earnings for their own. The experience of living without resources offers many opportunities to experience fear and to react with courage. Learning courage could help a middle class teenager stand against bullying. Learning courage could help an executive develop a multi-cultural workplace that values different ways of communicating. Learning courage can be an excellent gift from the wealth of poverty.

Resilience describes a state of being which exhibits strength, vibrancy and an ability to marshal emotional and spiritual forces to survive times of both challenge and joy. In the culture of poverty the joyous times are the ones to watch out for. Getting one's hopes up is often cause for the hardest of let-downs. Resilience is that set of qualities, developed over time, which allows for a return to normalcy after times or seasons of highs or lows. Every class strata can benefit from learning resiliency.

Adaptability is the capacity to change and to move through changes of circumstance. Often, the person in poverty has moved from home to home when the rent goes up, or family member to family member to avoid violence, or from job to job owing to hidden middle class rules. Adapting to change is a strength gained through experience. Adaptability is the key to future innovation. Innovation is not generally planned. Organizations can benefit by learning a capacity to change in a way that expects the unexpected to become manifest.

Patience is learned in the day to day pride swallowing siege that accompanies a life without or with little resources. Everything takes longer. Waiting for busses, waiting for services at government offices, and waiting for charities and religious institutions all take patience. Waiting for activation days and waiting for paychecks also require patience. Medical care takes hours and sometimes weeks to find without insurance or a job. The myth that hospitals and emergency rooms can't turn people away is only believable if one does not live among the poor. This learned patience would be helpful to adopt if one faces frustration when waiting in traffic or at the grocery store. This strength is also very helpful in learning to spend hang-out time with neighbors.

Tolerance is the competence to endure adverse conditions without breaking. In the case of the culture of poverty, adverse conditions can be environmental, physical, emotional and/or psychological. Environmentally, the poor are expected to live in cheaply built, poorly insulated housing with unrepaired water issues that yield mold, and insect and rodent issues, among others. Heating and air conditioning can be ill maintained or ineffective, if there was money for utilities at all. Many lower income jobs are out of doors in heat and cold. Physically, the culture of poverty includes limited access to health care and body pounding jobs, including long hours, heavy lifting, standing or working with dangerous products. According to the Centers for Disease Control, Asthma prevalence was higher among children, females, and those with family income below the poverty level, and differed by race and ethnicity for the period 2008–2010.[15] Adverse emotional effects are tied to physical well being and increased by the effects of poverty. "Both individual and neighbourhood deprivation increased the risk of poor general and mental health. Poor people in poor neighbourhoods reported more financial and neighbourhood problems and rated themselves lowest on the ladder of society."[16] JD Herrera, Director of Trinity Ministries at Parker Lane UMC in Austin, TX captures the sorrow of the poor neighbor when he says, "We believe that crappy things will always happen to us and we think we deserve it, someone has to deserve it and we are the low individual and so we receive the worst." Adverse conditions in poverty far exceed that which can be described here. Suffice it to say that tolerance can be learned from experiencing intolerable conditions. Tolerance can become a wealth of the ruling class by learning from the experience of poverty. Tolerance is the precursor of peace, acceptance and understanding, all of which are valuable commodities.

The strengths gained by the poor through the experience of poverty can be valuable and can be learned. Persons holding to the status quo may not initially see the beauty beyond the difficulty, but it is well worth the time to mine these strengths for the kingdom of God.

---

15 http://www.cdc.gov/nchs/data/databriefs/db94.htm, 9/4/2013.
16 Stafford M, Marmot M; Synopsis of: Neighbourhood deprivation and health: does it affect us all equally? International Journal of Epidemiology. 2003 Jun;32(3):357-66.

Not-So-Simple Wondering

1. The authors list the strengths that are instilled through experiences of the culture of poverty as 1) Loyalty, 2) Courage, 3) Resilience, 4) Adaptability, 5) Patience and 6) Tolerance. Each of these strengths look different to middle class eyes through the crucible of poverty. What do these strengths look like in your community?

2. Choose one or two of the strengths listed. How did your understanding of that strength develop? If you were to talk with someone in poverty about that strength, would you be talking about the thing? Or would you be talking past one another? How could you bring the two closer together?

CHAPTER 5

The Wealth of Valuing the Less Valuable

Talia just got a call from her baby's daddy telling her that their daughter, Maria, wouldn't be home at the end of the weekend. His car was having problems again, the bus fare was $80 to send her home, and he was overdrawn. He was certain he could get Maria home sometime next week when a guy he knows could be by to fix his car. He also felt certain that he will be able to afford the parts with the money he will save on child support since Maria will be staying with him. Talia's friend from work is honking for her in front of the house. They had planned to ride to work together today. Frustrated that she didn't budget money for this kind of BS from her ex, she heads off to work at her $2.13/hr job waiting tables.

Halfway through her shift, Talia gets a table of four, a very Picky Lady and her family. The daughter is very unhappy. It seems as though her teenage existence will be completely ruined if she can't have the new purse they just looked at in the mall. Picky Lady and her husband are fighting over parenting styles. Picky Lady complains at Talia about everything on the table, orders a $50 bottle of wine, gives her daughter $100 for the purse and the keys to the car to go get it. Little brother heads to the mall with his pouting sister who doesn't want to be a taxi for the wimp while Picky Lady and Dad settle in with the wine. Great! Now Talia won't be able to turn this table over for more tips. It is the perfect end to a perfect day. Her daughter is trapped far from home, a problem that would *cost less than a spoiled girl's purse, and Talia is powerless to do anything about it.*

— From *Stories of the Congregational Wesleyan Church*, 2009

As early as 1738 CE, mathematicians were attempting to quantify the subjective nature of value. Daniel Bernoulli, father of the fluid dynamics theory which makes carburetors and airplane wings possible, accomplished research proving logarithmically that perceived value is affected by individual psychological factors. Bernoulli proposed that maximum expected usefulness is affected by perception of personal gain, not only monetary gain, but also gains based on psychological biases. Further, the effect of monetary gain on this logarithm has diminishing returns based on the amount of money a person already has. [17] To clarify, the value of money diminishes based on the amount of money one has.

If the value of money diminishes, what holds value? It is important to understand how value is determined in order to define what holds value. Hosts of interdisciplinary scientists continue working toward defining the X-factors that will effectively predict human decision making as regards valuation. Sales people rely heavily on this research to convince buyers where to invest hard earned resources. Political activists hope to be able to predict your decisions at the polls. For now, experts and theoreticians generally agree that value is assigned by rational human beings based on four factors: cognitive ability, avoidance of negative emotions, effort required, and possibilities for rationalization.

Cognitive ability is marshaling the complete group of mental processes necessary for completion of tasks, including thinking, remembering, doing and etc. Howard Gardner defined eight modalities required for cognition which he labeled "intelligences" (the label generated controversy, the idea is generally accepted). [18] Gardner's modalities are musical

---

17 English translation in Bernoulli, D. (1954). "Exposition of a New Theory on the Measurement of Risk". Econometrica 22 (1): 23–36.
18 From Frames of Mind: The Theory of Multiple Intelligences by Howard Gardner, copyright © 2011. Reprinted by permission of Basic Books, a member of The Perseus Books Group.

- rhythmic, visual - spatial, verbal - linguistic, logical - mathematical, bodily - kinesthetic, interpersonal, intrapersonal, and naturalistic. After a considerable amount of scholarly conversation, Gardner added existential and moral modalities as possibilities that he may have overlooked. With ten modalities to consider, cognitive ability is still art and science that remains a mystery in many ways. Due to the remarkable complexity of the human brain and its functioning, it is not possible, yet, to explicitly define how humans think through the process of valuation. It seems an obvious reality that people use their brains to decide worth and whether to pay the price, both rational and psychological, once worth has been established. As noted in Chapter 1, cognitive ability is measurably lowered by the stress of scarce resources. Those who are impoverished, then, begin the process of establishing value with diminished capacity. Added to the reality of destructive stress, Chapter 3 noted the adverse affect of chronic absence in kindergarten which led to stunted cognition development as late as the 5th grade. When cognitive ability is diminished, the competence to assess and compare value is diminished as well.

The second powerful factor in determining value is Avoidance of Negative Emotion. Imagine tasting the best chocolate in the world while standing in front of a bucket of ammonia. No matter how hard you try, the next time you think about chocolate, the memory of the ammonia smell is married with the memory of the chocolate flavor. The value of the chocolate will be determined in large part by the ability to control the desire to avoid the smell of ammonia. Many things that are valuable within a culture are valuable as they enable us to safely avoid negative emotion, or lose value because they are married with a negative emotion. Defense mechanisms like avoidance of negative emotion can be a powerful defense against pain, but, if overly rigid, can also create an unhealthy fear-filled psycho-pathology. Discussion of the avoidance of negative emotion as a defense mechanism of the human personality was first proposed by Sigmund Freud in 1894.[19]

19 Freud S. (1894). The neuro-psychoses of defence, in Selected Papers on Hysteria and Other Psychoneuroses; Trans. by A. A. Brill. New York: The Journal of Nervous and Mental Disease Publishing Company, 1912. Public Domain.

Negative thoughts, feelings, and situations are not the problem. How people respond to these negativities is the cause of the psychological distress. Although everyone has negative experiences that may create pathological responses, a person who learns family violence, hunger, and living with little or no protection from heat and cold holds a more immense potential for assigning value based on avoidance of negative emotions.

The third factor in determining and assigning value is how much Effort is Required. Making decisions is costly. Often called Cognitive Effort or The Cost of Thinking, the idea that thinking and deciding requires effort and too much effort expended results in negative feelings was first presented publicly by George Mandler in 1982.[20] Stated simply, it isn't easy to place a value on an item or moral position and then decide to pay that cost. It is easier to stick with known quantities, alleviating the need to expend the effort of deciding or of changing. How much effort is necessary to determine the value of an item or position determines how likely persons are to feel good about, and pay the cost of, that item or position.

The final factor in assignment of value is the ability to Justify a Decision. Justification means to show sufficient reason and is a fantastic tool for protection of the individual and that individual's right to choose. It is important to be able to rationalize the cost and benefit that was utilized in the making of a choice. Particularly when cognitive dissonance occurs, when one is uncomfortable with a decision that has been made, justification allows space for self-survival. In order to establish a system of value which places some things in preferred states and some things in less preferred and some things in not preferred categories, one must be able to justify pushing some things out of the favored place of value. Without the ability to justify and rationalize a person would be unable to stand by and maintain a system of value.

The cognitive and personality factors discussed above are marshaled to process rationalization and justifications for human decisions. Since

---

20 Mandler originally presented his idea publicly under this title: The structure of value: Accounting for taste by G. Mandler, edited by: Margaret S. Clark, Susan Fiske In Affect and cognition: The seventeenth annual Carnegie Symposium on Cognition (1982), pp. 55-78.

assigning value is a decision which is always subjective, many levels of processing are going to be active at the same time. For those who are armed with the rules of polite society, these decisions and the value assigned by these decisions may seem obvious. For those who struggle with deciding how to get to work without a car and without money, for those who have been beaten and raped since age six, for those who operate in the matriarchal, relationship-oriented culture poverty provides...these decisions of assigning value may be nigh onto impossible.

Considering all the factors that affect what humans value, the questions become extremely difficult to answer. What is valuable in the culture of poverty? The middle class? The culture of wealth? Ruby Payne organized information on what is valuable in each of the three cultures. Some questions derived from Payne's research and instructional program follow.[21] Payne uses these questions to allow participants to see their own ingrained cultural biases, in effect, to examine the waters of the cultures different persons swim in by pointing out the values embedded within each cultural aquarium.

---

21 From Crossing the Tracks for Love, by Ruby K. Payne, 2005. Excerpted from A Framework for Understanding Poverty Workbook by Ruby K. Payne © 2012 aha! Process. Permission to reprint.

Could you cope with a spouse/partner who came from old money (or had that mindset)?[22]

It would bother me if my spouse or partner:

☐ Spent money on private club memberships.

☐ Had a trust fund from birth.

☐ Insisted on the artistic quality and merit of household items, clothing, accessories, and so on.

☐ Had a personal assistant to assist with purchases of clothing and accessories.

☐ Spent money on a personal tailor and physical trainer.

☐ Spent a great deal of time on charitable activities and did not make or take money for that time.

☐ Placed our children in the care of a nanny.

☐ Insisted that our children be placed in private boarding schools at the age of six.

☐ Talked a lot about the presentation of food.

☐ Staffed and maintained homes in more than one country.

☐ Spent money on a private airplane and/or yacht.

☐ Established trust funds for our children at birth.

☐ Maintained social and financial connections with individuals whom I didn't like.

☐ Had family members who looked down on me because of my bloodline or pedigree (or lack thereof).

☐ Kept an accountant, lawyer, domestic service agency, and investment broker on retainer.

☐ Was adamant about details, insisting on perfection in virtually everything.

☐ Wanted to have nothing further to do with a decent individual who didn't have a suitable connection.

☐ Spent $1 million-plus on an original piece of art, and would only purchase original works of art.

---

22 From Crossing the Tracks for Love, by Ruby K. Payne, 2005. Excerpted from A Framework for Understanding Poverty Workbook by Ruby K. Payne © 2012 aha! Process. Permission to reprint.

- ☐ Attended an Ivy League college or university.
- ☐ Valued me largely for my social connections.
- ☐ Reviewed family assets and liabilities on a monthly basis.
- ☐ Purchased furniture and furnishings for their artistic merit or designer designation.
- ☐ Kept almost no food in the house.

Could you cope with a spouse/partner who came from middle class (or had that mindset)?[23]

It would bother me if my spouse or partner:

☐ Spent long hours at the offi ce.

☐ Required our household to run on a budget.

☐ Planned out our week in advance.

☐ Started a college fund at the birth of our child.

☐ Hired a plumber to do a needed repair.

☐ Fixed the plumbing himself/herself.

☐ Played golf every weekend with his buddies.

☐ Kept a job that he/she hates for fi nancial reasons.

☐ Rigidly adhered to time demands—and was oft en early.

☐ Was organized, keeping a paper trail on everything.

☐ Refused to give money to relatives who weren't working.

☐ Refused to allow a relative to come live with us.

☐ Planned vacations a year in advance.

☐ Spent evenings taking graduate courses.

☐ Devoted considerable time to a community charitable event.

☐ Shopped for high-quality clothing/shoes/accessories, then charged those items.

☐ Withdrew TV, computer, and other privileges from the children as part of discipline.

☐ Paid for our child's college expenses and tuition.

☐ Paid for tennis, golf, dance, swimming, and other types of lessons for our child.

☐ Oft en made a big issue over the quality of food.

☐ Bought reprints and numbered artwork as part of our home's décor.

☐ Purchased furniture for its practicality and match to the décor.

☐ Had family members who discounted me because of my lack of education or achievement.

---

23 From Crossing the Tracks for Love, by Ruby K. Payne, 2005. Excerpted from A Framework for Understanding Poverty Workbook by Ruby K. Payne © 2012 aha! Process. Permission to reprint.

Could you cope with a spouse/partner who came from generational poverty (or had that mindset)?[24]

It would bother me if my spouse or partner:

☐ Repeatedly gave money to a relative who would not work.

☐ Left household bills unpaid in order to give money to a relative.

☐ Loaned the car to a relative who doesn't have insurance and cannot be insured.

☐ Allowed a relative to move in and stay with you.

☐ Didn't pay attention to time (e.g., missed dates, was extremely late, didn't show).

☐ Quit jobs without having another one because he/she didn't like the boss.

☐ Cursed at his/her boss in public.

☐ Physically fought—fairly frequently.

☐ Didn't think education was important.

☐ Left items in the house unrepaired.

☐ Used physical punishment on the children as part of discipline.

☐ Viewed himself as a "fi ghter" or a "lover" who works hard physically.

☐ Served food from the stove, and ate most meals in front of the TV.

☐ Almost always had the TV and/or radio on, and oft en loudly.

☐ Kept the house dark on the inside—poorly lit and with window coverings closed.

☐ Kept organizational patterns of household chaotic.

☐ Bought clothing from secondhand stores, garage sales, and so on.

☐ Bought designer clothing or shoes for our children, but didn't pay an urgent household bill.

☐ Made a big deal about the quantity of food.

☐ Viewed me as a possession.

☐ Had family members who made fun of me for having a college degree.

---

24 From Crossing the Tracks for Love, by Ruby K. Payne, 2005. Excerpted from A Framework for Understanding Poverty Workbook by Ruby K. Payne © 2012 aha! Process. Permission to reprint.

☐ Bragged about me by talking badly about me.

☐ Chose to spend time with relatives, rather than spending time with me.

☐ Purchased alcoholic beverages for entertainment before paying for necessities (e.g., car insurance, utilities, rent).

Payne's questions aptly illustrate the differences between the culture of poverty, the middle class gatekeepers and the wealthy benefit. In the middle class culture money is managed, personality is a job aid for success and self-sufficiency is the watch word for living. This is the foundation for the hidden rules that operate in work places and schools. The poverty class has hallmarks of value for relationships and entertainment, as does the culture of wealth, but wealth has a social principle of exclusion that is not present in either of the other cultures. A closer look at what holds more value in the culture of poverty will be useful here.

Scarcity and vulnerability teach people to depend on one another. Relationships become the primary unit of value. Resourceless individuals can finish long work days and still have the strength to go help someone move because relationships are survival. Eric, a high-functioning autistic man, can play guitar in worship because, more than anything, the poverty stricken church members want to connect with him. Generational Poverty can value the less valuable, as defined by the ruling classes, by valuing the beauty in things other social classes may not even be able to see. The value of relationships is a cost most definitely counted in the culture of poverty and will be explored in the next chapter.

Not-So-Simple Wondering

1. In Talia's story at the beginning of the chapter, she needed $80 to get her daughter back while the Picky Lady paid $100 for a purse. Which is more valuable: $100 to the Picky Lady or $100 to Talia? List as many causes as possible for the discrepancy. Will the Picky Lady and Talia ever be able to understand one another?

2. Think about your last major purchase. How might the four factors of determining value have effected your decision to buy? (cognitive ability, avoidance of negative emotions, effort required, and possibilities for rationalization)

3. Consider Ruby Payne's chart. Are there any surprising entries on the chart? In which group do you find the majority of your answers? How different are your answers from those that grew up in generational poverty? Is there anything held valuable in the culture of generational poverty for which you wish to develop more value in your own life?

CHAPTER **6**

The Wealth of Networking

Most winters, I slept in the corner of the 24-hour Winchell's Donut House in Upland, CA. Around 4:30 or 5 each morning, the owner would let me eat a couple old doughnuts before the morning crowd came in for the fresh ones. He would make sure that I was up in time for school, which was just across the street. I somehow felt that he started waking me up to make sure that I was out before business got going in the morning, but over the course of time, I felt more like he cared about me surviving, even if only on a couple of doughnuts. I never invited my friends to join me there and I never asked for anything beyond what was offered. I guess I just coveted a warm night's sleep in the wintertime.

I travelled once to another city, following the hope of a great job where being twelve and homeless wouldn't matter. The hope was too good to be true and I found myself alone and hungry in a less-safe-than-Winchell's environment. A church was advertising a free meal, so I walked 18 blocks for warmth and food. When I got there, I was handed some ill-fitting clothes and pointed to a shower line. Apparently, clean clothes and a free shower were part of the free stuff the church was offering. Too bad I overheard one of the church ladies commenting on how much easier the rest of the evening would go after we didn't smell so bad.

After we all showered, we were ushered into the sanctuary where a long-winded preacher told me that all my problems were the result of my bad choices and if I would only choose Jesus tonight, everything would change. The kid next to me told me that if we went up front and started praying, the preacher would quit talking and we could get on with eating. After three days without food, I was completely ready for the eating part, so I went up to the altar, knelt down and prayed. It wasn't at all hard for me to pray. I have known Jesus through many dangers, toils and snares. Family violence, drunkenness and homelessness all provided me opportunities to depend on the boundless love of my Lord Jesus Christ. What I was less sure of was whether or not the preacher's notion of my "bad choices" had anything at all to do with me. I was not sure that I could pin down a time when I had a choice.

Anyway, one of the women at the altar began to weep and the rest of us stole away quietly to the back for some hot food. It was a great feast with soup and bread and casseroles and Jell-O in more versions than I could ever remember before. I was warm and full and beginning to feel quite human, when, suddenly, the evening was ended. We were given our newly washed clothes, asked to return the clothes we were given on arrival, and ushered out, back into the streets.

I started to walk back the 18 blocks, when it occurred to me there really wasn't anything in particular to go back to. It was a cold night and I found a heating grate, a vent where the furnace of a hi-rise building releases steam so I curled up there. Pretty soon a transvestite hooker paused as she was walking past and asked if there was room for two. I just shrugged. A few moments later, I was wrapped in the arms of someone who needed me as much as I needed a friend. I slept, warm, full and loved. Not such a bad day, after all.

When I awoke the next morning, my new friend and I went off to find a place to hang out. I wondered then, and still wonder now, who really was the face of my Jesus that day. Was it those who focused on showers, thought I had choices, and turned me out into the night? Was it the one who kept me warm as I adjusted to night life without Winchell's and then befriended me in the light of day? I still don't know for sure. I'd like

to think both groups reflected something of Christ, but my heart leans
toward the transvestite as the one living Immanuel, Christ with me.

—Adapted from "Faith Stories in the Congregational
Wesleyan Church" (2008)

It is time to face an important reality: People leave churches for reasons. Some of them are really good reasons: Persons in leadership have
behaved dishonorably toward persons in their care. Persons in the pews
have allowed themselves to become imprisoned by their own comforts,
giving just enough to make the building and ministry serve their own
likes and dislikes. The Church has determined that a particular behavior is
worthy of disqualification (speaking out against power mongers, divorce,
alcoholism, abortion, homosexuality). People leave churches for reasons.
Some of them are really good reasons. These reasons make it difficult to
speak to "The Church" about The Wealth of Networking which is fully
and completely about relationship. The best place to start then is with the
admission, compared to God's ability to love, we are all the impoverished,
trying to relate with those who are poor.

Relationships built in scarcity of resource are often misunderstood
outside the culture of poverty. The atrocious things educators (based in
middle class culture) tell one another about children developing in these
environs are almost unforgiveable. A Google search for "relationships in
poverty" yields 51,000,000 results. The first several pages of the search
are educational reports, often with impressive footnotes, which state family relationships in poverty are horrible. The problem with accepting this
assessment is the definition of family that is used and the assumption that
all impoverished families parent badly at all times. Family is an extend-
able concept in the culture of poverty and is the number one resource
available to those imprisoned in that culture. For instance, a child in poverty may have a mother who is a whore for those who will provide her
Crack Cocaine (read crack whore/bad parent when using), but also has
a grandmother who prays for her daily and an uncle with a home where

she lives with her brother, six cousins and a homeless couple they met at church. Due to the blended nature of these families there will be intercultural and interracial relationships as well. It does not feel like a sacrifice to share a bedroom with 6 persons of limited means or a different skin color or language in these extended families. Gathering with an extended family, eating whatever was found or earned that day and taking in a TV show or two can fill even the most horrendous poverty with joy.

Relationships in resource scarce communities illustrate at least three basic Christian behaviors which were present between Jesus and the twelve disciples who became apostles; joyful community, recognition of unjust systems and intercultural/interracial mobility. Examining Jesus' relationships on earth may yield better understanding of "on earth as it is in heaven." (Matt 6:10 NRSV)

Extended families are the most effective conduit of care for the impoverished around the world. Guy Scott, Vice President of Zambia, Africa, said; "[W]e believe that extended family system still remains a critical component in our society as we try to alleviate poverty and uplift the well-being of others."[25] The extended family forms joyful community, recognizes unjust systems, and experiences intercultural/interracial mobility in actual practice. A closer look follows.

The requirements for joyful community are to love God and love one another, often called the combination of the Great Commandment (Love God) and the Great Commission (love one another). Extended families in poverty look a great deal like Jesus and His disciples. The sick, the poor, the orphan, the crippled and the faithful joined one another to the glory of God in the Holy Land in 30AD. They lived together, learned from Jesus together. They found healing together. They ate together. They fell in love with God together. Dr. Kyung Chik Han, speaking to the Asia-South Pacific Congress on Evangelism in 1968 said "The early Church, their hearts were filled with joy, for they were at peace with God and men. They were happy, for they loved God and one another. Such a joyful

---

25 Available at: http://www.postzambia.com/post-read_article.php?articleId=31909, 25 April 2013.

community attracts people, just as a beautiful flower garden attracts butterflies and bees. Such a church grows daily, naturally and without much conscious effort." The extended family can look like this today. There are certainly exceptions when it doesn't, but it may be time to stop holding up the exception to avoid participating with those who are the rule. God's love is being lived out in extended families in poverty every single day and it seems a great tragedy that the hidden rules of the middle class create fear which keeps people from experiencing this love. When there is nothing to eat and no resources to fall back on, knowing that there is a group of people to bond with who are experiencing the same situation is priceless, joyous, and a very attractive and beautiful flower garden.

When an extended family with no resources is the flower garden which attracts people, injustice is easy to see. One definition of injustice is benefitting while others starve. The ability to recognize unjust systems may seem obviously simple, and yet, recognizing injustice is one of those simple but not easy cultural quandaries. People generally believe they can tell the difference between right and wrong. Nelson Mandela pulls society up short though when he is reported as saying: "Massive poverty and obscene inequality are such terrible scourges of our times – times in which the world boasts breathtaking advances in science, technology, industry and wealth accumulation – that they have to rank alongside slavery and apartheid as social evils."[26] In the Hebrew Bible, Nathan had to go tell David a parable that proved it was a bad idea to steal Uriah's wife and order Uriah to be left for dead (2 Samuel 12). Tamar had to impersonate a hooker to propagate the family line of Jesus when her father-in-law, Judah, violated the law of family relationships (Genesis 38). Humans are effectively clueless at seeing their own error, especially errors that put people at odds with their own moral code.

The Twelve Disciples who surrounded Jesus couldn't see the limits of their cognitive prisons either. Jesus was always correcting them. Jesus knew that humanity was living in a framework where layers of sacred

---

26 http://africa4green.com/on-poverty/. Accessed 10-12-2013.

violence were necessary to reach the central worship space of the Jewish Temple, called the Holy of Holies. This framework needed to be displaced and God chose to allow one last act of sacred murder to pull humanity's head out of its cognitive imprisonment. At the Communion table, Jesus substituted himself as the sacrificial lamb. There would no longer be a need to temporarily paper over separation from God. Rather, this final abuse of the system set by the Torah would be the undoing of the entire sacrificial system which is now replaced by divine generosity of self-offering love. Cognitive prison opened, the disciples went out and changed the world. Even though Jesus knew of the unjust nature of murdering the innocent to save the guilty, it took Him three years of working within the system to train His disciples to see it.

Injustice is far flung in the world of achievement, greed and selfishness that is built by the culture of power and supported by its middle class. Systemic injustice or individual injustices may be difficult to recognize, but there are a few keys to look for which may help open the cognitive prison door. The World Bank has provided resources for a great deal of research among the poor around the world. In "Voices of the Poor," a World Bank study on what people in poverty believe about their situation, the authors found: "Poor people...describe poverty as the lack of food and assets, the powerlessness that stems from dependency on others, and the helplessness to protect themselves from exploitation and abuse because of their dependence on the same groups for survival."[27] Briefly stated, food, assets and powerlessness are the hallmarks of poverty according to the impoverished. To determine one's level of participation in the culture of power, simply become aware of the food, assets and power under your control. Comparisons from that point will help adjust perspective. The average US woman owns 17 pairs of shoes; the number of barefoot orphans in Africa is above 20 million.[28] A coffee at Starbucks is $2.98; two injections of Nevirapine costing $2.00 will prevent transmission of

---

27 Narayan, Deepa; Raj Patel, Kai Schafft, Anne Rademacher, & Sarah Koch-Schulte (2000): Voices of the Poor. Can Anyone Hear Us? Oxford University Press, The World Bank, p.266.
28 See www.shoes4souls.org.

HIV to the newly born child of an infected mother.[29] Cash, relationships, abilities, education and jobs are all assets in the world economy. The culture of power will consider these assets disposable while the culture of poverty considers them blessings. Power knows whom to lord it over. If you feel someone is beneath you, it may be a good time to stop and consider how to extricate yourself from the role of oppressor.

Recognition of unjust systems is a prerequisite for operating successful networks. Injustice takes advantage of participants, both those oppressed and their oppressors. Injustice puts people, both oppressed and oppressor, at odds with the desire of God's heart for human communities: love God and love one another. Unjust systems isolate participants in the culture of power from those in the culture of poverty by instilling a feeling of deserved rewards in one and removing any hope of the power to succeed from the other.

Interracial/intercultural relations are prevalent in the networks of the culture of poverty. Just as disciples came from all over Israel, Capernaum, Chorazin, Tiberias and Judah, the mobility of the culture of poverty ensures that the people moving through the community will also come from all over. Many communities, where people own their houses or farms, are much more sedentary than the culture of poverty. Jesus moved from city to city and town to town. The culture of poverty moves with the work, food and resources. There are great benefits to living around new people every day or week or month, whether the movement is your household moving, or persons moving through your house. Learning to be around people of many races and cultures is challenging and refreshing and expands the knowledge and temperament of the individual. In addition, more people means more resources to pool, which is always a good idea when resources are scarce.

---

29 An excellent explication of these costs can be found online at: http://pmtct.org.za/docs/
nevirapine.php or in print: Skordis, J and Nattrass, N. 2001. What is Affordable: The Political
Economy of Policy on the Transmission of HIV/AIDS from Mother to Child in South Africa.
Paper presented to the AIDS in Context Conference, University of the Witwatersrand, April
2001.

On the dark side: Interracial and intercultural issues can remind impoverished people how unjust the world can be. One of the men in the following story is a member of a local Austin, TX congregation and one of the men is a family member of a friend of the congregation. Both men are roughly the same age. The similarities stop there.

"John" is an African American man born in rural Texas to a family that is from generational poverty. Raised in a large family, John was loved by his family. He found good employment and had some success in his relationships. And he developed an addiction to alcohol. He has been arrested three times for DWI and for associated charges while he was intoxicated. When he was arrested the third time for DWI, he was considered a "habitual offender" and was awarded a felony conviction. He served several years in prison and is now out. John is sober, fully employed with secure housing, and is an active and vital part of our congregation.

"Bill" is a White man born in rural Texas to a family from wealth. Raised in a typical "nuclear" family, he was well loved. He went to college (as was expected), attended medical school, married and became a successful physician with an active practice. And he developed an addiction to alcohol. Bill has had three incidents involving alcohol. The first resulted in the major destruction of property. The second resulted in injury to a person on his own property. The third involved a single car accident that totaled a car. There have been police inquiries at each of the events, but Bill has not been arrested. He has never been charged. Bill has quietly paid for the damages out of his pocket so Bill's insurance hasn't even been affected. Bill is still practicing medicine and still has a problem with alcohol.

The difference between John and Bill is vast. There is certainly an economic difference between the two men. Where Bill has been able to buy his way out of trouble, John has not. However, there is also a skin color difference and that has made all the difference. It is not only the economic advantage that has "shielded" Bill, but it is also his skin color. Although police have responded to some of the damage that Bill has caused, Bill has never been arrested. Bill has never been charged or finger printed.

This story is hard to evaluate because there are two factors to consider; race and economic class. The racial concerns are heightened by location: Austin, TX, USA. Austin has a population of folks who want to be "post-racial" – their claim is that there is no longer racism in the United States. However, they are white. White people don't get to say when racism is dead – the privileged only get to listen. Listening though, is a truly great way to experience the wealth of poverty. Learning how to live in interracial settings is a fantastic way to learn to become post-racist. The privileged class is not there yet, but the culture of poverty can envision and enact post-racism as something familiar that is already a fundamental within the extended family system.

There is reason for gratitude. Some recognition exists that racism is still an issue in the United States, and a group of people exist who believe all persons, regardless of race are indeed created equal, even in the United States. Intercultural realities hold out less hope. Those who are economically secure have been taught the myth that those who are not economically secure are "lazy" or "victims." A true intercultural, multi-class approach is to see all people as the extended family of God, acknowledging that the circumstances of poverty play havoc with even the most competent people.

The extended family system of the culture of poverty offers the wealth of networking in much the same way as Jesus and His early disciples; loving God and loving one another in joyful, interracial and intercultural realities which recognize and overcome injustice. Anyone is welcome to participate in the extended family system. Big Brothers/Big Sisters participates in meaningful ways with kids who might otherwise lack role models. This level of participation, hanging with kids after school, or an even deeper commitment, cooking dinner and watching TV with the family twice a week is doable. If finding the culture of poverty is difficult, just ask the teachers at a local school, they know the cultures their students are living in. Once poverty is found, begin to network by sharing, first, your time.

Not-So-Simple Wondering

1. Identify the hidden rules in our church gatherings. List as many
   as possible. Consider appropriate entry, exit, seating, greeting
   etiquette, and subjects of conversation that are acceptable
   and unacceptable. How did you learn the rules? What are
   the consequences for breaking the hidden rules? How does
   knowledge of the rules affect your ability to network?

2. Think back to the story of the child who visited the church for
   food. If you could speak to a person in the story, who would
   it be and what would you say? If you could ask one of them a
   question, what would you ask?

3. How does the culture of poverty excel at networking? How
   might learning from those with few resources benefit people in
   the Middle Class or in the Culture of Power? Is it possible for
   the Middle Class or the Culture of Power to learn from those in
   poverty? If so, how?

CHAPTER 7

The Wealth of True Reliance

I have been to Guatemala three times in the past two years, and I have seen poverty with my own eyes. I have seen what it is like to not have shoes. I have seen what it is like to not have a stable house to live in. I have seen what it is like to not have enough food to eat, and I have seen what it is like to not have clean water to drink. However, I have also seen all of those needs met, and have been a part of meeting those needs. Although poverty exists in our world, we are not without hope. I have seen villages in Guatemala completely transformed and I was completely transformed as well. Villages that did not have homes, clean water, a school or a church now have all of those things relationships that I could never have imagined I now have. This could not be accomplished without communities of people coming together. In all of the villages that I have visited, the physical needs are the most obvious...I can see that they do not have clean water, do not have enough food, and do not have stable homes, but what cannot be physically seen is our need for God and our need for people. Meeting physical needs is great and extremely important, but there is nothing like looking into the eyes of a woman with children and grandchildren to feed and telling her that God loves her and that she is not forgotten; not forgotten by people and certainly not forgotten by God. I have had the opportunity to physically put shoes on children's feet. When I was in Guatemala in August of 2013, I went to a village with my team and all the kids from the village lined up for their new pair of shoes. They came up one by one, took a seat in front of me, and I washed their feet. How humbling it is to sit in front of children who cannot defend themselves against the cruelties of culture with nothing but a bar of soap. After washing their feet, I placed the shoes on them. The joy in their eyes after receiving their shoes was incredible. I wish I could know gratitude so deeply...and for the simplest things. It is an experience I will never forget.

There were two things that impacted me most on that trip to Guatemala. The first was putting shoes on bare feet, and the second was developing a relationship with a thirteen year old girl who was living in an orphanage. She clung to me right away when I met her and she began telling me her story, without me even asking. After she finished telling me her story, she asked me to keep it a secret. Only a few people knew what she had gone through as a child. I felt honored that she would trust me with her story, and I felt incredibly grateful to God for bringing the two of us together. Because she lived in an orphanage, she had all of her physical needs met, but was in need of a friend, especially in that moment, and I believe without a doubt that God specifically placed me in that situation to be the friend she needed at that time. At the same time, I believe God made her the friend I needed when I was far from home, new to the culture and in need of the security of a feeling of purpose.

—Lydia Brunelle, The Cause Community Church, Brea, CA

Poverty is the absence of vital resources. Much more than the absence of money, poverty is the absence of food, clean water, shoes, jobs, health care, friendship and hope. In this crucible of lack and want, the culture of poverty forges the wealth of true reliance. There is no doubt whatsoever in the minds of the poverty-stricken masses that dependence is real and abiding. Impoverished individuals must rely on God and humanity to provide the resources that are necessary to maintain life. This is not reliance on others for provision of luxuries; this is reliance on others for water that doesn't make a person sick and calories sufficient to sustain the human body, health care, friendship and shoes. In Chapter 1, research was presented which proves scarcity of resources diminishes people, but learning reliance on a community can reinvigorate growth and hope for the individual. True reliance is a way of life that recognizes, through a community, needs will be provided for in the same way the birds and flowers are dressed and fed (Matt 6).

Just as poverty is more than a lack of money, true reliance is more than dependence. True reliance is interdependence. Building a network of resources to meet the onslaught of needs requires relying on one solution for transportation, another for rapport, a pastor for translation skills, a free clinic for health care, a school for lunches, a government program for affordable housing, the neighbors for the TV antenna, and a missionary for shoes. Lydia, in the story that begins this chapter, speaks in the middle class voice, and yet, the young girl in the orphanage could see something in Lydia that was worthy of interdependence. That young girl could see that Lydia has been through the crucible of a culture without resource. Lydia has experienced a culture of poverty of her own, seen poverty "with her own eyes", and learned how to be open to alternate strategies to meet her own needs and the needs of her family and extended family.

Assembling a team sufficient to meeting the level of impoverishment requires relying on self and God rather than hiding behind resources. Reliance leads to a deep belief in something bigger than self — even if that "something bigger" is not connected to a church. Impoverished persons have come to believe that churches might have resources that can sustain life, even if only for one evening and then back to the streets, but government agencies and extended families can be accounted as "something bigger" than self as well.

Albert Einstein said, "The positive development of a society in the absence of creative, independent thinking, critical individuals is as inconceivable as the development of an individual in the absence of the stimulus of the community." As humans, we are all interrelated and need to rely on one another to become all that we are meant to become. Resources, and dependence on resources, isolate individuals from community, thereby hampering the community's ability to grow. A community without growth stunts the growth of the individuals who are reliant on that community. Therefore, just as the absence of resources diminishes individual potential, the presence of resources diminishes community potential. Communities are formed by engagement with individuals, who are offered the opportunity to participate in activities which then produce sharable commodities.[30] When the individual has sufficient resource to remove themselves from communal participation and production of sharable goods, the individual, with no community correctives, becomes self-centered and small. Perhaps this is one point of significance for God's immense valuation of the poor. Relationship and community are valued above all in the culture of poverty, freeing the individuals within that culture from the limits of resource driven self-centeredness. In addition, if Einstein's thinking is accurate, failure to join a community dooms any attempt at helping that community to thrive. People from the culture of power, no matter how well intentioned, cannot intervene in the culture of poverty unless they are fully engaged within it. A donation of dinner or the clothes your kids are done with, while providing short-term crisis management, is insufficient to the task of inter-reliance necessary for mutual growth.

The Wealth of True Reliance is interdependence. Communities are formed by engagement with other individuals, who are offered the opportunity to participate in activities which then produce sharable commodities. Failure to fully participate in community diminishes the individual and failure of the individual to participate diminishes the community. Interdependence allows for the mutual growth of all persons. True reliance, then, leads to the mutual growth of all persons. Resource rich individuals may consider at this point that the "what's in it for me" question is, by its very nature, indicative of the self-centered modality that diminishes community. Resource rich individuals who wish to experience

---

30 Further reading on community formed by identity through activity has been written by Etienne Wenger. (1999). Communities of Practice: Learning, meaning and identity, Cambridge: Cambridge University Press.

true growth in community (true reliance) will find it necessary to spend time in community with those who have the wealth that resource scarcity provides. In order to learn reliance, resource rich individuals need to go into the schools in the poverty stricken neighborhoods and attend classes with impoverished students. To achieve the growth only community can provide, one must stop trying to buy away the struggle and start participating in the production of sharable goods, which one must then share.

True reliance is paramount to understanding God's manner of being and God's expectation for human being. Interdependence can only be learned by living in community as equals, and this depth of reliance is present in all facets of Biblical identity. The Tri-Unity of God, three persons dancing in one essence (Google "Perichoresis" and the "Council of Chalcedon" for more information on the Doctrine of the Trinity) can only be experienced from a human perspective in a community of interdependence. God created the community of Israel by setting apart a holy people and entering into covenant relationship with them. The Apostles gave an example of interdependence by travelling the world and encouraging all believers to share their lives and belongings as the way to glad and generous hearts. True Reliance is the interdependence that allows humans to grow in godliness.

Not-So-Simple Wondering

1. When was the last time you truly had to rely on someone else to meet your needs? What feeling dominated that time? Were your relationship needs cared for? Did your resources cushion the experience?

2. If you had to rely on a community, who would you turn to? Would they let you sleep on their couch? And if so, for how long? Would they still treat you the same? Who would you let sleep on your couch? And for how long?

3. "True reliance... leads to the mutual growth of all persons." What are the dangers of interdependence and sharing in the community of poverty? What might you learn and how might you grow? Is it worth the cost?

Closing Remarks

MAN is born free; and everywhere he is in chains. One thinks himself the master of others, and still remains a greater slave than they.
— Jean-Jacques Rousseau[31]

Everything we own actually owns us. The poor are exponentially wealthy because they depend less on things and more on God's Favor, A Cohesive and Identifiable Culture, Imaginative Scheduling, Experiential Strength Development, Valuing the Less Valuable, Networking and True Reliance. Learning these riches is tantamount to understanding **Matthew 19:21.** "Jesus said to him, "If you wish to be perfect, go, sell your possessions, and give the money to the poor, and you will have treasure in heaven; then come, follow me."" We want for everyone who reads this text to find Jesus' kind of freedom by capitalizing the wealth of the culture of poverty in your own life. We want for all who encounter this argument to realize that accessing the wealth of poverty is finding true freedom, freedom from locking your doors and fearing your neighbor. The wealth of poverty offers us all the ability to take care of our needs and the needs of our families without incorporating the need to overuse, steal from others or leave children hungry in order to buy extra shoes or fancy coffee.

If we have made this argument compelling, then you are now longing to establish a relationship with the culture of poverty. The truth is that, if you picked this book up in the first place, you already had a heart to

---

31 Rousseau, Jean-Jacques. 1762. The Social Contract. Translated by G. D. H. Cole, 1923.

help the poor. You've probably been doing mission work for at least some of your life. At the end of this book, we assume that you have already figured out that relationships across economic groups will change you, and that makes sense, since God is in the business of transformation. We are praying that you are ready for transformation. Keep in mind that actual transformation will require more effort than a "six-week course." The Bible is filled with relationships and relationships are the model for transformation (in Jesus life on earth and beyond it). Relationships are the primary currency of those in generational poverty. Since we assume these truths, we won't offer a program to help you get started. Instead, we invite you to ask yourself some simple questions...

How much time are you willing to invest in this process? Think about the last time you formed a friendship. How much time did that take? Does it make sense to think here in terms of weeks, month or years?

Are you willing to let God guide you in establishing life-transforming relationships with those in a different economic group? Are you willing to worship at a church on the poor side of town for two years? Are you willing to mentor weekly? Are you willing to participate in interdenominational groups in order to introduce you to people who are different than you are?

Are you ready to let God transform your life for the good of you and of the community? The culture might be telling you that you are "all good" but that might not be the whole story. What are you afraid of losing (because you might lose it)? Can you describe a time in your life when you were afraid of losing something but God ended up bringing you something amazing instead of the thing you wanted for yourself?

Remember, Jesus said, "I am with you always even to the end of the age." (Matthew 28:20) You are not in this alone. Recently, the Pope reminded us, "This church with which we should be thinking is the home of all, not a small chapel that can hold only a small group of selected people. We must not reduce the bosom of the universal church to a nest protecting our mediocrity."[32] Feel free to contact either of the authors if you run into a snag in your transformation journey. We are interested in the difficult and rewarding transformational work that God does in all of us. We are willing to work hard to exceed our own mediocrity. We are willing to let ourselves be vulnerable and be changed. How about you?

---

32 Pope Francis, in an interview with Antonio Spadaro, S.J., translated in America Magazine, Vol. 209 No. 8, Whole No. 5023, 30Sept2013.

Appendix 1

These stories are being provided to you so that you can read, pray, ponder and perhaps use them in an ongoing study. These are real stories from our neighborhood. We have changed the names to protect the identity of our people.

Each story is coupled with some "not so simple wondering" questions. They might be suitable for Sunday school, for leadership prayer, for personal reflection or just as a way to learn the language of poverty (which is primarily story).

These stories were written by Tina Carter except where noted. They were originally written in an informal voice as a means of developing relationship between our primarily generational poverty church and a primarily middle class church. They are not in the academic vernacular and they often switch between first person and third person voice. They were written over the course of a little over a year. We have done fairly little editing where these stories are concerned and so we beg your indulgence as you read through. Use the ear of a listener and treat them as the informal stories that they were created to be.

You have permission to copy these stories, and when you copy them and use them in your church please encourage people to write the stories of their own lives.

Access to Healthcare

"Colleen" has a delightful personality, and is very helpful. She has raised three grown children who are a real gift to the community and has a 10-year old who is a very helpful and gifted child. Colleen worked most of her life and for over 20 years her employer provided her with good health insurance. Unfortunately, Colleen got very sick and was diagnosed with Lupus. She lost her job and, after three months, her health insurance as well. She is now working on a very part time basis and working hard to make sure her family is okay. Her youngest child's father has a job in construction but that income is not constant and neither of their jobs carries health insurance.

Here's what happened recently. Colleen lives right outside the Austin city limits and broke her arm. She went to a local hospital emergency room where they took an x-ray, confirmed that she had chipped her elbow and then splinted her arm (her arm was too swollen to cast). They told her to come back on Monday to get a cast. When she returned on Monday, they told her that, since she didn't have insurance or the cash to pay for the cast and because she lived outside the city limits they couldn't help her. They directed her to another agency in an adjoining county to apply for an "indigent care" card. She did, but was denied. A medical doctor, who is a friend of the church, called to try and get her services but couldn't. She went to St. David's Medical Center because she had been assured that they could help and would schedule payments for her treatment but that wasn't true. Once again she was turned away. After about three weeks of this she knew something was really wrong because the pain had not abated in any way and in fact was getting worse. She went back to the hospital but they thought she was just seeking pain medication so they sent her away. Eventually she found a doctor who took pity on her, and against all the rules, took off the temporary cast and found that the pain was caused by a skin infection which had increased the swelling. He cleaned the wound and treated the skin but still couldn't cast it. He re-splinted her arm and sent her on her way. Her arm took a long time to heal and we still aren't sure it healed correctly.

Not-so-simple Wondering:

1. In the current system, would you describe health care as a privilege or a right?

2. As people of faith, who should have access to health care in our city? In our country? Internationally?

3. What would need to be done to bring the two views more closely in line, both here and abroad?

Single Parent

"Earl" is a single father of three children - two boys and a girl. He's been raising them on his own for a long time. Now, of course, Earl must work full time to support the kids and he is finding that difficult especially since he doesn't have childcare. He finally found a job that allows him to work while his kids are in school but he still needs a couple of hours of care for them after school. All kids are good kids, some just need a little more coaching and Earl's oldest needs a little more coaching. As he was meeting with the counselor at the elementary school once again, he mentioned that he was at the end of his rope and explained the lack of care for his kids and the fact that he was trying to manage on his own. The counselor called the local United Methodist Church, and said, "please help." Earl came over to enroll the kids in an after school ministry. One of the single dads whose children are mostly grown came over and encouraged Earl. He recounted the difficulty he had experienced and the deep need to have a community to support you if you are trying to do this on your own.

Sunday morning Earl showed up with his three kids in tow. They ate breakfast in the gym before worship. People remembered their names. The single dad that had encouraged Earl earlier in the week sat by him in church. Other single dads from the congregation greeted him and let him know that he wasn't alone. Earl and his children are now semi regular attenders on Sunday mornings. Difficulties still arise. Earl's kids do not know and/or always follow the rules at church and at school. The congregation strives to encourage a man who has stepped up to the plate and be a community for children some would label "irredeemable".

Not-so-simple Wondering:

1. How did the school know they could call the church? What would it take to build that bridge with a local school?

2. How does a church grow healthy boundaries with the children? When the kids act out, what consequences would be helpful for their development?

3. What does Earl need? Can the church provide it? Could your church provide for the needs of Earl and his children?

Why Haven't You Been to Prison?

"Blake" was driving home children from an event. "Stephanie," a ten-year old full of questions, asked him, "have you ever been to prison." Because Blake takes Matthew 25 seriously, he was able to tell Stephanie that he had visited both jail and prison. Stephanie, in an exasperated voice said, "No! When have YOU ever been to prison?" When he replied that he had never been, Stephanie looked quizzically at Blake and asked, "Why not?

Not-so-simple Wondering:

- ❖ What do the children in your neighborhood think "everyone does"? How does the culture of poverty effect Stephanie?
- ❖ What might a conversation between Blake and Stephanie look like in 5 years? In 10 years? In 20?

Homeless Families

Mom, Dad and baby in stroller showed up at the church for help. In their native Spanish, speaking to a Native Spanish speaking congregation member and the pastor who understands Spanish but speaks only English, they told their story. The dad had come to town for work and had brought his family because he loves his family and wanted them to be safe. They were invited to stay with a friend of the family in the apartment complex behind our church. They came with their baby and their three other children. Everything was fine at first — his works was good and steady and their friends were enjoying having them there. Then everything fell apart. His job ended and the next job didn't show up. The apartment complex told his friends that if they didn't kick out their guests then they would be evicted.

Not-so-simple Wondering:

1. What do you suppose the church did? What would your church have done? What would you do?

2. How many things had to go wrong for the family to be homeless? Many Americans are only two paychecks away from being homeless. What things would have to go wrong for you to be homeless? What resources would you have to draw on? If you were evicted from your housing, what feelings might you feel?

Redemptive Employment

"Mark" is in his twenties and he has some incredible skills as an artist. His talents are the envy of many and include strong skills in lettering, drawing portraits, and sketching landscapes. His art has a stark and wonderful beauty. Although he is in his late 20's, Mark has already spent over 10,00 hours on practicing his art.

Mark is also a recovering heroine addict and an ex-offender. He has recently been released from jail. That can be a difficult transition, especially when you have been incarcerated for multiple years. The rate of developing technology today makes you a stranger to so much. In addition, there are very few prospects to get into housing (most apartments will not rent to you if you have a felony record) and very limited job prospects. For ex-offenders, this is a recipe that usually ends in relapse and a return to prison. In addition, if you have spent most of your young adult life incarcerated, and you come from generational poverty it is difficult to gain the confidence necessary to believe that any life, other than a life of failure, is what is destined to be your lot in life.

However, a local church knows and loves Mark. They have experience with addiction know about boundaries and encouragement. They know about coaching and understand that when you coach someone who's confidence level is already low, grace is going to have to be the primary currency.

The church wrote a grant for redemptive employment. The total grant of $1,000 was funded and enabled them to hire Mark at the church to manage some projects. They met with him to talk him through his employment contract, helped him to fill out a W-4 form for the first time in his life, and made it clear that they were in this for the long haul. They stuck with him when he missed meetings and let him know that, like the hounds of heaven that God sends after us to chase us down so that we can receive God's grace, they were not going to let up. They are now only 23 hours into that employment (over a period of 4 weeks). And so far here's what's happened: 1. He's redesigned the church logo so that it's updated and impressive in it's artwork. 2. He's made contact with a local screen printer and is working with them to get that logo transferred to bags so that they can sell them in the congregation, 3. He's designed the summer camp t-shirt logo, 4. He's gotten a sense that he can do this work, 5. He's admitted that, "at the beginning I didn't think I could do this because I've never done anything like this before but now I think it's easy."

He is dreaming about how to get an artshow together and where it might show. He's learning how to make "limited edition prints." He's already dreaming of how he might make his own line of T-shirts. He sees himself in a different light. The truth is that he may not get to finish out his employment at the church because he may find permanent employment before the small grant is finished. That would be a true gift from God.

Not-so-simple Wondering:

1. Jesus asks us to visit the imprisoned. (Bonus points if you know where that Scripture is.) Is prison visitation part of your churches visitation ministries?

2. What does it take to progress someone from prison to employable? i.e. time management, self-esteem, technical training, work-place behavior, etc...

3. What are the dangers of becoming involved with ex-offenders? Why might God require us to overcome those barriers?

Houselessness

"Jimmy" is a 40 something who worked construction all his life. He felt secure because he had a good job, a nice apartment and had even amassed savings. And then his appendix burst. Once he was recovered, his medical bills and his lack of income had helped him run through most of his savings. He wasn't too worried because he knew he could work again once he was recovered. However the construction company where he had worked for many years said he was a medical risk and so he didn't have a job. He lost his home because he had no money. He found employment and is working hard now, sleeping in the streets and showering at a local church. He figures that in another 6 or 8 weeks he'll have enough money to get into an apartment.

ꙮꙮ

"Nellie" was a professional, middle class woman who had always worked and had always done well until the economy tanked. She lost her business. She had a hard time finding a job. Once her stress increased she also got ill and that stopped her job search. She still wasn't worried because she had credit cards to get her through. Once those were maxed out, she lost everything. Without stable housing or resources she ended up on the street — alternating between friends houses and the street. Now employed, she got a room at a fleabag hotel so she could have a roof over her head. She spends the night on the street some nights in order to save more quickly to try and get into an apartment.

ꙮꙮ

"John" is a 60 something man who worked hard his whole life. He even worked at churches. Now arthritis has set in (his hands show the clear signs of that disease). He has some small income (a little over $300 a month) because he has now been classified as disabled. He can't work. He knows that within a year, he'll get Social Security which will allow him a little bit more a month — enough to maintain at least a roof. He got into a rooming house, but the rent is more than what he has. So he's headed back to the streets until he can "get some more age on him."

"Dorothy" and "Elizabeth" are both mothers. One has an infant and one has an elementary aged child. In both cases, their significant others left them, without resources, without a home, without options. Because the women were not "beaten," they are not eligible for the help of anti-abuse organizations. They have the challenge of trying to get themselves and their children to a safe place while they deal with being abandoned. Dorothy and Elizabeth are both trying to figure out what God is doing for them next.

Not-so-simple Wondering:

1. Many job applications and housing applications are now online. Questions are asked such as your current address and phone number. How might one of the people mentioned above fill out an application?

2. When you go for an interview, many employers expect a certain level of dressed up. As one of the people mentioned above, where would you find the clothes for your interview? How would you get them washed? How would you get to your interview?

3. As people of faith, what can we do? What are we willing to do?

Encouraging Advantage

Fifth grader "Jenny" decided that she wanted to apply to the Ann Richards school (www.annrichardsschool.org) - a public school for young women grades 6 through 12. This school is designed to develop young leaders and is based on several successful all-girl school models. The school specifically invites young women who come from economically disadvantaged areas to apply. The goal of the school is to allow these girls some of the opportunities that you might regularly find in suburban schools and middle class cultures.

But Jenny didn't decide to apply until the weekend before the application was due. She and her mother knocked on "Mabel's" door on a Saturday morning asking for help. Mabel is an active member of the community and known to help others. In order to apply, Jenny needed to write an essay about why she wanted to go... in English. Spanish is her first language and her mother speaks only Spanish. They all went to the church to use the computer. Mabel spent a little over an hour working with Jenny and her mother to get the essay written. It was a difficult process because Jenny had to teach her mom a little English and Mabel a little Spanish so that the adults could communicate. Finally, the essay was finished. The last line of the essay read:

You should let me into this school because I want to go bad enough that I made my mom go to church on a Saturday so that I could write this essay.

Not-so-simple Wondering:

1. What do you suppose made Jenny want to attend the school? How did she hear about it? How might others learn of the opportunity?

2. Imagine other times Jenny might have to translate for her parents. How might that effect the parent-child relationship? What other results might come from the translation?

3. What opportunities might come from attending the school? What difficulties could Jenny face at the school? How can her church help with the transition?

The Language of Faith

Matu is the native language of Mam, a man who immigrated to the United States five years ago from Myanmar (Burma). He is employed full time, is connected to a community and is a Christian. He has attended worship at our church more than once and we know him by site, and now by name.

He asked for an appointment with the pastor. When that happens you never know what you are going to hear. Sometimes folks are trying to make sure that they are heard. Sometimes they need prayer. Mam wanted to talk about his community. He is a member of a Christian community here in the city. He worships with a larger group that speak in Burmese, the official language of Burma, his native country, but not his native language. He made it clear that some of the people in his group (of about 45 people) could understand Burmese, though some could not. Although they share a country, they do not share a language and it is common (apparently) for there to be some tension between groups. He was approaching the church to see if we could find space for his group to meet to study and pray in their own language. Because they are just a small group they don't have monetary resources as a group.

We met together and in his broken English and my non-existant Matu we listened to one another and I tried to get a sense for his story, his people's story and what they were hoping for. At the end or our meeting we went to the Sanctuary and kneeled to pray together. I prayed in English. And then Mam prayed in English too. I asked him if he would please pray in his native language. He said, "but you cannot understand my language." That's true I thought. And then I thought how often has Mam sat through a worship service or a prayer service spoken in a language that he didn't understand? And so, after I politely asked again, stating that I would be blessed to hear his language and the Holy Spirit could be trusted to translate the thoughts of our hearts, he prayed in Matu as we kneeled together at the rail.

As he was leaving, Mam looked at me and said that he was glad to have talked to me today. He said that he had been studying English and the Bible in English for two years in order to be able to talk to me about the possibility of having a space to pray in his native language. I was overwhelmed.

Not-so-simple Wondering:

1. Communicating across language barriers is not easy or quick. Describe a time when you had to communicate across a language barrier.

2. How does language play into poverty? What solutions do we offer?

3. What do you do with your building besides on Sunday morning?

Prostitution

"Shawna" showed up at church with a man that gave everyone the creeps. We were fairly certain that Shawna was turning tricks in our neighborhood (that is, that she was working as a prostitute in our neighborhood). While she was there, we gave her good, honest work, and worked alongside her. We praised her work ethic as we washed dishes together. We reminded her that God loved her and wanted for her a future with hope. Without shaming her, we acknowledged that the way she was surviving wasn't actually giving her life. Less than a week later we were not surprised to hear from her male "friend" that she had been arrested. He was asking us for money for her bail. We saw this as, perhaps, one of her few routes to escape him. We didn't give him money because we knew (by checking the arrest record) that she couldn't be released anyway. He was going to pocket any money he could get.

Not-so-simple Wondering:

1. What might have led Shawna to turning tricks? What obstacles might she face extricating herself from prostitution? Would you hire someone with an arrest or conviction for prostitution?

2. List the times Jesus met with prostitutes. How did he react when a prostitute showed up at his ministry? What he would have done if her pimp had showed up?

3. How Jesus-y are we in Christian ministry?

These Shoes Aren't Made for Walking

"Mary" walks to all her 3 jobs. At least some portion of her day is taken up by walking. She uses the bus to make the long hauls but buses don't drop you from door to door. In order to get to one of her jobs, Mary walks about 3 miles because that particular job is three miles beyond the last bus stop. It takes her about 45 minutes to complete the walking portion of her trip. The bus ride takes about an hour and 15 minutes. She is commuting two hours one way to get to this cleaning job where she is paid $50 to clean a house for a private woman. It only takes her about two and a half hours to clean the house and so the $50 seems like generous pay. However when you consider the travel time she has she is actually away from home about six and one half hours for that $50. (That's about $7.60 an hour — slightly above minimum wage but not the generous $20 an hour the woman who is paying her thinks she is paying.)

Her friends are encouraging Mary to let the woman know about her travel. The woman who hires her to clean her house is a woman of faith who has a sincere commitment to helping the poor. She just may not have an understanding of the day to day workings of the poor. Mary is reluctant to share the information. She likes the work and wants to support the woman because the woman does so much good for the community. Mary is praying about it.

It's not likely that the woman would ever notice the condition of Mary's shoes. Why would she? Thankfully, Mary's pastor did notice when she went to do a house blessing at her modest and wonderfully kept apartment. The pastor had walked to Mary's house because it was close. When the pastor saw the condition of Mary's shoes and realized the amount of walking she did in a day the pastor took off her own shoes (great, expensive black walking shoes) and gave them to Mary. She took Mary's shoes to walk back to the church.

The pastor walked two blocks in Mary's shoes before it became apparent that it would be better to walk barefoot than to walk any farther in

Mary's shoes. The pastor took the shoes off and walked back to church in her socks.

Not-so-simple Wondering:

1. Should travel time effect how much one is paid?

2. What does the public transit system look like where you live? Do you know how to make use of it? Where is the closest bus stop to your house? Could you navigate the public transit system, as a survival skill? Would you?

3. How many pairs of shoes do you own? How many of the shoes you own have not been worn in the last 6 months? What is enough?

Giving out of Abundance

"Bonnie" and her sister were students in an after-school program and both had long hair. Her sister heard the pastor talking about donating her hair to people who had cancer and said, "I want to donate my hair too." Bonnie was adamant from the beginning that she had no desire to donate her hair. Everyone assured Bonnie that that was okay. The pastor made arrangements for Bonnie's sister to get her hair cut at a downtown salon.

The day came...

And Bonnie's sister changed her mind. The after-school program staff and the pastor assured her that it was okay. Sometimes we change our minds and God loved her no matter what. At that moment, Bonnie decided that she did want to donate her hair — after weeks of insisting she was not going to.

The experience was amazing. Bonnie was nervous and brave. Her mom was proud. Her sister ended up regretting not taking that brave leap. In the end, Bonnie saw herself as a child of God capable of helping her neighbor.

Not-so-simple Wondering:

1. Bonnie ended up giving out of her abundance. What are other valuable gifts the "poor" can donate in order to participate in the Kingdom of God?

2. What do you have that you could give?

3. Do you believe that God could change your heart about generosity the way that Bonnie's mind was changed about donating her hair? What might God have to do to convince you?

4. In what ways was Bonnie leading in her community as she donated her hair?

About the Authors

"Reverend Doctor Tina Carter in 50 words: child of God, wonderer, daughter, mother, wife, pastor, scientist, engineer, writer, teacher, philanthropist, coach, storyteller, addict, recovering, hiker, walker, nature lover, friend, fun enthusiast, eager learner, listener, pattern recognizer, reader, expert knitter, trainer, strategist, hairball-orbiter, & according to the best sources: awesome grandmother."

"Rev. Dr. Mindy Johnson-Hicks, Congregational Wesleyan pastor, lives happily in Austin with her wife Amy. For 15 years, she served churches as mentor, pastor and crisis communications director. She authored two books, three church operations manuals and designed leadership protocols for several church systems. Mindy's family has experienced grinding poverty for generations."

CPSIA information can be obtained at www.ICGtesting.com
Printed in the USA
BVOW08s1349160415

396257BV00005B/31/P